MW00574028

"The eye of a quiet outs
Tzu astray among southern Connecticut industrial decrepitude, finding empty landscapes, empty time—perhaps some great rage and sorrow held at bay by the immaculate measures of poems that are certain of, if nothing else, the rhythm of their own closure, so that the quiet feeling that the poetic measure realizes also develops poignant observations into poignant reflections: 'the warm sun / of early fall / falls forever / through the long afternoon.' These poems, tinctured with a very special sadness, offer innumerable sensitive recoveries of moments that are, miraculously, also left alone: 'lost / under a blue sky / in an eternally / forgotten landscape.'"
  —Charles Stein, author of *Persephone Unveiled*

"For someone so quintessentially gentle and sensitive like Jonathan Towers, perhaps a place where the earth is increasingly smothered by asphalt and concrete, where the air is increasingly polluted by electronics, where the sea is increasingly choked with mercury—for someone like Jonathan, all this may have proved insupportable for sustaining the kind of life he needed. My wish for Jonathan is that he may find himself beside a pristine tumbling mountain stream, barefoot, and sing to himself, low and and unharassed, that most lyrical of lines of Chuck Stein: '... *and wash / my feet / in sassafras leaves.*' My affection to you always, Jonathan."
  —Tek Young Lin, retired school chaplain, English teacher and cross-country coach, Horace Mann School, Riverdale, New York

WESTPORT POEMS

Jonathan Towers

North Atlantic Books
Berkeley, California

Published by
North Atlantic Books
P.O. Box 12327
Berkeley, California 94712

Cover photo: Jonathan Towers and his older brother Richard
Grossinger with their mother, Martha Towers, Westport, 1951 or 1952

Cover and book design by Paula Morrison
Printed in the United States of America

Westport Poems is sponsored by the Society for the Study of Native Arts and Sciences, a nonprofit educational corporation whose goals are to develop an educational and crosscultural perspective linking various scientific, social, and artistic fields; to nurture a holistic view of arts, sciences, humanities, and healing; and to publish and distribute literature on the relationship of mind, body, and nature.

North Atlantic Books' publications are available through most bookstores. For further information, call 800-337-2665 or visit our website at www.northatlanticbooks.com.
   Substantial discounts on bulk quantities are available to corporations, professional associations, and other organizations. For details and discount information, contact our special sales department.

Library of Congress Cataloging-in-Publication Data
Towers, Jonathan, d. 2005.
   Westport poems / by Jonathan Towers.
      p. cm.
   ISBN-13: 978-1-55643-595-9 (pbk.)
   ISBN-10: 1-55643-595-9 (pbk.)
   I. Title.
   PS3620.O93W47 2006
   811'.6—dc22

2006015327

1 2 3 4 5 6 7 8 9 UNITED 12 11 10 09 08 07

Thanks to Norma Brown, Kassandra Brown, Danielle Brown, and Jed Bickman for keyboarding this book.

We would also like to acknowledge the following donors to this publication: Stephan Rechtschaffen, David Squires and family, Tek Young, Lin, Stephen Ritchin, Gail Elson, Lee and Bea Aschen-brenner, Stephen Heller, Arthur J. Jacobson, Emile Pincus, Joe Green, Richard Huttner.

Collection One

Poems 1995–2001

SILVER SANDS STATE PARK

July 5, 2000
(Milford, CT)

scatter
of low
shed-like buildings
& the isolated run
of telephone poles
like masts
tilted in the wind
leaping wires
like rigging
alone
in an immense stretch
of open
unbroken wilderness
under huge skies
like somewhere
in East Texas

Rowayton Station
September 30, 2000

only a tin can
rolling
in the empty
parking lot
of the empty
railway station
in the light breezes
of a sunny
saturday afternoon

variegated woods
& thick vegetation
hide an adjacent street
of suburban homes . . .
the blue sky dominates . . .
lines of empty railroad track
fade around a bend
in the distance

SWEET WILLIAM

February 7, 1997
(Antiques & Café)

we pass the time
in idleness
in a candy-colored setting
johnny mathis
croons sweet nothings
the day disintegrates
behind lace curtains

there should be
nothing on the mind
epicurean freedom
from turmoil
the world & its problems
drowned in aesthetics

SASCO CREEK
September 20, 1996

it was just before
the fall equinox
middle of an afternoon
we strayed thru weeds
out onto the marshes
soggy at high tide
in brilliant sunlight
wild wind
animating tall reeds
& grasses

across the creek
on a spit of land
where the creek forms
a small outlet lake
three cormorants
perched in the dead arms
of an old haunted
barepole
candelabra-shaped tree
looked like carved ebony
indistinguishable
from the branches
they were a part of
works of nature
turned to art

three cormorants
made a message
of themselves

in an old dead tree
they are the tripartite world
one is land
one is sea
one is sky . . .
and the dark time
time of autumn gold
is on its way

HEMLOCK RESERVOIR
September 4, 1996

we clambered uphill
thru horse farm country
crossing and recrossing
at odd intervals
the upper reaches
of the creek
climbing a ladder
to the sacred reservoirs

steadily mounting
following a map
of quiet roads
hacked out of forest
joining others
in a zigzag ascendance
to the oracular waters

finally downhill
across a more-traveled road
flanked by old hemlock woods
dead branches
breaking at our passage
to the shallow edges
of a miles-long lake
strangely devoid of life
cupped in hillside forest
stretching north and south
thru Indian wilderness

AFTER LABOR DAY

sea gulls
like blown pieces
of paper
congregate
for bread crumbs
in the parking lot

the beach house
is closed
for the season

in the motionless morning
telephone strands
hang limp
down the empty road

WALGREENS

August 10, 1996

world
of
dead objects
and
mass-produced
gimcrack
culture
carried on
under the
fluorescent
hypnotism
of a
weatherless
fishbowl
hermeticism
for the exchange
of
no longer precious
metals
and
the lifeless
products
of
factory-made
industry

MEMORIES OF LONG BEACH

July 27, 1996

by the walls
    of old sea ruins

old faces
    cracked & preserved
        by
        sea
        wind
        &
        sun

    rosebushes in backyard gardens
always the sand invading from the beach

        brown weathered slats
           &
        sea-rusted handrails
           of
           the
           boardwalk

and the lonely look
    of empty sand dune lots
before the lonelier look

    of the empty ocean

MACHAMUX

May 4, 1996

3:30 a.m.
i gaze into the nocturnal territory
of the cat
prowling the housegrounds
thru pine &
mixed-hardwood
forest
drenched after the long day's rain

THE RETURNING TIDE

July 12, 1996

Burial Hill Beach
peninsulas of mud
Greens Farms, CT
exposed
at the tidal mouth
bleary-eyed dawn
reflected
in the cool shadows
of the creek water

out at sea
a thin haze
is lifting
& the world
is revealed
thin-streaked
in pastel tones

i walk along the shore
on the blank tablet
of morning
red glow
in the east
beyond trees . . .
i've come back again
on the returning tide
of another day

SEA SCENE

July 1, 1996
Greens Farms, CT

pastel blue sea
white haze
on the horizon
a few scattered sailboats
low wash
of the receding tide

the cormorant
airs his wings
the gull
wades in the shallows
the egret
picks his way
among the rocks

along deserted beaches
in the declining afternoon
we wander
on the very most edge
of a continent
amazingly
as though 1000 miles
lay between us
& anywhere

Morning Poem

March 10, 1996
Greens Farms, CT

in the immaculate
morning
i'm afraid
to disarrange
a pebble
on the shore
of the universe

the oyster shell
i chuck into the sea
thinking it might live
should have been left
for the gulls

in the face of immensity
i break down
in triviality
backed against the sea wall
i watch the gulls
carry on the work
of creation
wading in the morning shallows

The Mayor of Darien

September 18, 2000

the "Mayor"
is street-smart
observing back-alley
truck deliveries
& other developments
under the shade
& protection
of a parked car
in the tiny lot
beside the pet shop

the "Mayor"
is on call
throughout the day
receiving clients
either inside
or at his outside office
recommending aimlessness
as antidote
for a purpose-driven
citizenry
advising loitering
for a fast-paced world

beloved by all
the "Mayor"
takes his popularity
in stride
success has never
gone to his head

election time
finds him unprepared
as usual
but the results
are always the same:
a landslide victory
in every voting district

TOKENEKE BROOK

May 26, 2000
Darien, CT

i glimpse
between homesteads
the quiet drift
& meander
of Tokeneke Brook
shaded in vegetation
symbolically placed
in the background
of the moment

we stand always
at right angles
to another reality
the life
we can't see
looks back at us
& in the pastoral ideal
of the brook
reveals
a right-angled projection
of our deepest possibilities

THE MAYOR OF DARIEN

i think of him
posted outside the pet shop
reclining in his basket
or shading himself
in the shadow
of the telephone pole
or maybe wading
through his weeds
or wandering down
the alley-like street
out on an adventure

i think of him
when i'm miles away
in another town ...
of the balanced
and circumscribed
orbit of his world
like the patterns
in a sage's life
one is trying to emulate

THE MAYOR OF DARIEN

imperturbably
he observes
the daily traffic
about him
from the vantage point
of his basket-centered retreat
the motion of birds
and occasional squirrels
as significant
as that of humans

purposeful activity
passes to and fro
before him
with long lulls
in between ...
with mayor impartiality
he views it all
and thinks nothing of it

in his perfect detachment
the world is reduced
to its constituents
form color & movement
are separated out
and recombined
in the higher unity
of his speechless philosophy

SOX & COMPANY

February 7, 2000

strange mockery
of the human voice
from the cage
hidden in back
tropical colors
and faraway jungles
in the time-stopped world
of the pet shop

the cat sidles
down the narrow aisle
toward the front door
the parrot
preens himself
in the looking glass
of his curtained parlor

outside
in the common world
of pigeons & crows
Darien's "mayor"
lies in his basket
with toy fish
receiving the affection
of the town

THE CAT
April 20, 1997
(Pelé)

behind the evergreens
and the garden
the cat
stalks his prey
in the evening
just after sunset
in observable moonlight

turns his eyes
like searchlights
on the terrain
wild hunger
loose among the flowers
belly-deep in grass

the intensity
of his concentration
amazes me
here is the animal
more than any other
watching and listening
and keeping still . . .
all the skills
of a chess player
all the wisdom
of a philosopher

THE BRIDGEPORT BLUEFISH
June 16, 1998

smoke drifts up
from smokestack chimneys
from beyond right field
beyond where the trains
can look in
as they slowly curl
thru downtown Bridgeport

city of old factories
old northeast center
of heavy industry
city of immigrant labor
that knew Barnum & Bailey
that knew the Depression
& World War II
and grew
and declined
suffering crime & corruption
& bad drugs

through which flows
the dirty Pequonnock
across marshes
out to Long Island Sound
city of old iron
railroad bridges
that now
in the last years
of the century

hosts a minor league team
in a new-build ballpark
in the fledgling Atlantic League

while the stars fall
through the falling night

HARBOR YARD STADIUM
June 19, 1998

offshore thunderstorms
reverberate in the distance
the strangeness
of the approaching solstice
paralyzes the suspended landscape
late-evening sun
clears the lower regions
of a mottled sky
throwing thick
snake-segmented bands
of golden light
on towering smokestacks

rock 'n' roll music
broadcast over speakers
thrills the evening air
then intervals of comparative silence
while the game slowly approaches
its beginning

snake-long commuter trains
coil lazily beyond
outfield fences ...
on the breezy parapet
the incoming throng
shuffles into the welcoming arms
of the collective occasion
the skies of evening
bless the ritual ground below

Bridgeport at home
against the Newburgh
Black Diamonds
the Bluefish take the field

honored at tonight's game
are finally shown their seats
in the third inning
by officious ushers

professional baseball is here
back in Bridgeport
after years of famine
the umpire's voice
bellows into the megaphone
of the night
STEEERIKE ONE

HARBOR YARD STADIUM
June 25, 1998

Captain Sounder
B.B. Bluefish
the Newark Bear
and a host
of other loveable mascots
garbed in fantastic
animal costume
shake hands
bestow hugs
and sign autographs
while delighting
the children-filled crowd
with their crazy antics

the panoramic vision
of an industrial city
surrounds us
the ferry departs
for Long Island
the commuter trains
make their evening runs
cars & trucks
ceaselessly pour
east & west
over the uplifted interstate

in the center
of a mandala
stands the horseshoe-
shaped stadium

encircled by perpetual motion . . .
a foul ball
caroms off a wall
in the upper tier
I pounce on the treasure
holding it aloft
to the cheers
of a chorus of fans
it's my first live souvenir ever
and i grasp the ball tightly
making sure of the reality
letting it sink in deep

THE GAME

June 28, 1998

on the other side
of the Housatonic
stretches the Azure Coast
(old pirate lair)
low-lying scrub
& marsh country
back of sand-white beaches

we explore by day
under summer skies
and in the evening
lured once more
by the call
of the ballpark
we depart the train
in Bridgeport
for another Bluefish home game
at Harbor Yard Stadium

3½ hours later
a near-capacity crowd
risen to its feet
wildly cheers on
reliefer Mike Guilfoyle
in striking out the last two
Black Diamond batters
with the bases loaded
in a tense
excitement-packed
3-2 Bluefish victory

GREENS FARMS

October 6, 1998

low tide
before sunrise
full moon
still in the west

balanced world
of sea & land
night & day

seagulls search
shallow waters
the low creep
of marshaled waves
signals the returning tide
ablaze in the east
beyond the wooded point
inferno
of the unascended sun

Greens Farms (Dawn)

January 19, 1999

the creek has flow
and twists past
miniature canyon walls
cut in nutrient-rich
mesa-flat marshland
thick with salt hay grass

down by the returning waters
of the Sound
the ancient origins
begin to take shape
beneath the auroral splendors
of an unseen sun
dramatized
by a long dark curtain
of partially-raised cloud

STRATFORD, CT
June 1, 1999

theatre
like a castle
in its airy bower
above the trees
with the wide rivermouth
behind it
and the riverside park
around it

old blocks of stone
from the dismantled
sea wall
hidden in vegetation
surmount the flooded marshes
of the river ...
sailing boats
tied at the wharves
near the bait & tackle shops

the theatre
that once boasted Shakespeare
is now defunct
a neglected
& unrecognized
national shrine
but the transplanted ghosts
of Elizabethan England
still haunt the empty park
declaiming against the silence

Taoist Meditation by Zen River

April 19, 1999

sound of the river's flow
enwraps us
in solitary freedom
sitting on the narrow
plank bridge
leading
to the miniature island

beavers probably once
dammed it
but now the water
runs free
sparkling
in april sunlight
divided by the island

here are upper reaches
of a river
we've only known
as tidal
here are earlier stages
in the river journey
of our lives
fallen like old sycamores
to sprout new roots
in dark river soil

HEADING WEST
April 21, 1999

the men
standing round
the truck
looked up
and saw it too:
a wild turkey
marching down the RR tracks
in the middle of the day
headed west

vast distances
stretched before him
his clawed feet
clattered
from tie to tie
as he pressed forward
determinedly
head bobbing
throat gobbling
seeming almost human
in his comprehension
of railroads

i said
"he's headed for Chicago"
and my friend called him
a hobo turkey ...
there was a moment

when we all watched
caught between
the amazing
and the ridiculous

The Dregs

even in the most sophisticated
towns
even in the most prosperous ones
where everyone commutes
and lives in a fine home
and has more than one car
the white trash element
can be found
bragging of its barroom adventures
its mind and body
bloated with poisons
puerilely fixated
on the gross
the vulgar
the crude
and the obscene

attached to pickup trucks
and the smell of exhaust
to all the toy-like gadgets
of modern technology
to nicotine and caffeine
and beer-guzzling orgies
foul language
bad food ...
sunk in juvenile depravity
over the slimy underside
of existence

it can be found
gathered at a local pizza place

or local garage
or gas station
lower than the low
subhuman almost
in its strange mockery
and rage and disgust
at its own condition ...
in its inarticulate absorption
with all of the baser instincts

TO A WORLD WAR II VETERAN
APPROACHING HIS 80TH BIRTHDAY
March 2, 2000

the distant echo
of the world-wide explosion
that called you overseas
lies dormant ...
collectively
we no longer remember
what it meant
to live in a world
at war

the other day
someone said:
"it was so different then ...
there was such pride
in the country"
and i looked
at this mind-mannered
photographer
forty years established
in his own business
and wondered
what it was like
to fly a plane
over Germany
in 1944

we live today
on the other side
of a cataclysm

the world survived
as it always must . . .
time has moved on
and the steps
that brought us here
are buried
in the archeological record

you are among those
who can still remember
a time
before the madness
we who live
in the ignorant aftermath
we who don't remember
still ask you
what it was like
to live in the flames
of a conflagration
that seared the whole world

Sox

February 15, 2000

with his wide tolerance
of other life forms
he seems to have
unconsciously imbibed
the ethic of the pet shop
and shares his meals
with birds & squirrels

in the prowling hours
of late night
perhaps he converses
with exotic birds—
strange discourse
in alien tongues
or else
totally ignores them

indifference
rather than tolerance
may explain him ...
like Puss 'n Boots
he's a cat
with a part to play
in the human world
and chasing birds
just doesn't interest him

DARIEN

January 14, 2000

the community
sits down to lunch
and a good rock 'n' roll
radio station
at Post Corner Pizza
New York City
is less than an hour
by train
there's no other town
along the shore
one need be envious of

in Tilly Brook Park
tall trees
benches & tables
diverging paths
& an open stone structure
surround quacking ducks
& geese
in a pond ...
traces of cliff-rock
from New York State
cut into
the Connecticut stratigraphy

Darien has nothing to prove
doesn't have to be anything
but itself
an American town

well-to-do
poised between New York
& New England
satisfied to be itself
nothing more
nothing less

"Sox"

November 6, 1999

after the train
leaves me off
in downtown Darien
I go over
to see the "Mayor"
usually resting
in his basket
by the entrance
to the pet shop

or if it's still morning
he may be in his weeds
among the foxtail grasses
in late summer & fall
beside the tiny vacant
grass-grown lot
just beside the store

grey and white
short thick fur
with patches of white
on his face
and under his chin
and more on his feet
from which his name
SOX

many come
to visit the mayor
to pass a word or two
in the middle of the day
and move on ...
and the mayor
is always friendly
has the sweetest disposition
and gets reelected every year

MILFORD

September 26, 1998

the pirate island
sits offshore
accessible on foot
at low tide
a stranded iceberg
turned to woods

surrounding us
low-lying scrub country
overrun by wild grasses
drained
by reed-hidden creeks
indistinguishable from farmland
in the soft recessions
of distance

in the immensity
of the seaboard sky
the warm sun
of earliest Fall
falls forever
thru the long afternoon

Evening Poem

August 26, 1995
Burying Hill Beach
Greens Farms, CT

at sea level
the world extends
with our step
& we approach nothing

sun nears the end
of its journey
falling
though the bottled cloud
shadows absorb the light
the night heron
patrols the internal maze
of the tidal creek

our eyes look out
straining the distance
the trajectory of our lives
throws meridian lines
out to sea
our fishing hooks
grapple with infinity
we toss our words
on the pebble-strewn beach

here are the limits
of a world
that has no limits
you end where i begin

or vice versa
night picks up the failing day
sea replaces land
our eyes can see no further

turning inland
we head back along the creek
past the heron's fishing grounds
to the road that takes us home

EVENING POEM (2)

September 1, 1995
Burying Hill Beach
Greens Farms, CT

along the fringes
of day
we wander
slowly
downhill
to the sea
to where evening gathers
in the dark pockets
of the creek
sprawled in meanders
across the flattened landscape

gold-orange bars
of the sun
setting beyond Sherwood Island
& the last waders
the last fishermen
the last conversationalists

hanging out
at the fringes
of the world

burning gnats & mosquitoes
turn us homeward

thru the soft grey-green gloaming
past the dark earth-colored shadows

of the mudbank creek

white crane
& night heron

marsh elder
& sea lavender

& the broad sweep
of the tidal creek
bending
out of sight
into the mysterious invitation of night

EVENING WALK (5)

September 14, 1995
Burying Hill Beach
Greens Farms, CT

last stragglers
on the beach
at the end of summer
we wander
down empty sands
in the afterglow
of evening

multicolored clouds
in soft giant masses
spread across the firmament
long low indentation
of the coastline
extends in the fading west ...
sprawled shadows
of the mudbank creek
silently draining
towards the Sound

we say goodnight
to switchgrass
and scotch thistle ...
down the lonely beach road
over the stone bridge
we climb uphill
in the retreating daylight
into the shadows
of the lunar night

MILFORD/COLUMBUS DAY
October 12, 2000

the eyes
need new ways
new avenues of enchantment

we turn down
a street
we never have

five ponds
miniature Great Lakes system
woodland trails
in a nature preserve ...
lost
under a blue sky
in an eternally
forgotten landscape

The Grasses

May 25, 1996

stick figures
by the roadside
bobbing in the wind
arrow-straight reeds
jungle-tall
in the marshes
bearded soldiers of wheat
tasseled maidens of corn
endless acres
of prairie grass
high as the sky
in july
waving fields
of amber grain ...
out from under
the cover of woods
emerging from forests
marsh of the savanna
grasses & man
traveling the earth
in tandem

THE CHINESE RESTAURANT
August 28, 1997
Westport, CT

like Taoist monks

we sit an old fashioned
luncheonette booth
amid the bare symbolism
of unpretentious furnishings
sipping ceremonial tea
from handleless porcelain
stamped with sacred
calligraphic scenery
absorbing Chinese wisdom
from the singsong tones
and natural graces
of the owner & workers
borne eastward
above the banal chatter
of a shopping-center
American public

BURYING HILL BEACH AT DAWN
September 13, 1997
Greens Farms, CT

the tide has turned
& the returning water
flows back
up the carved canyon
of the creek
loop by loop
past a few herons
posted like sentinels
at intervals
along the banks

mists are rising
scattered clouds
are clearing
the rosy hues
of dawn
suffuse the light blue
pallor of the sky
the outline
of Long Island
begins to emerge
a faint yellow
hallucination
thru disappearing fog

the clear water
of the Sound
laps gently
against the red-tinged

sands of the shore
everything is fresh
& clean
the day after
the day
after
the rains

WESTPORT

December 9, 2001
(West Parish Road)

on the original map
we nestled beside the brook
& climbed uphill to church

present-day backyards
may obliterate
a former direct pathway

broken relationships
lie hidden
but future times
may reveal
the ghostly archaeology
we've submerged

BURYING HILL BEACH

September 11, 1997
Greens Farms, CT

New Creek
& Mill Creek
merge
at the end
of their short
meandering runs
& flow together
into the Sound

the land
in back of the coast
is sea-level low
scattered woods
intersperse
the marshes

when i first came here
i was impressed
by the flatness
the tides
the big sky
& the land's end
nature
of the era

now
several years later
the distant

mountainous interior
is a myth of escape
that doesn't exist ...
one lives by the coast
having just made it here
& no more

BEACH SCENE
September 7, 1997
Greens Farms, CT

empty beach
early sunday morning
the returning water
laves the shore
the sun
is already warm
the gulls
cry out
standing on low-tide rocks
or dipping
in short diving arcs
over the water

facing the eventlessness
of space
i lose all desire
drifting like a sailboat
i have no direction

Old Saybrook

June 6, 1998

after the long day
of sunshine
the train up here
the afternoon exploration
of town
and rivermouth
and the walk back
along the Sound
across the marshes
over Back River
in the declining light
to find
the casual excellence
of the restaurant
its charm
of unpretentious elegance
then to speed off
into the night
to the railroad station
lonely as a whistle-stop
in the gathering perfection
of the crescent moon
waiting
for the last train out

GREENS FARMS

April 27, 1997

the untroubled waters
of the Sound
lie perfectly still
in early morning
Sunday calm
the parabolic coastline
curves east and west
in huge scalloped arcs

i stand in the shadow
of the seawall
looking out
at the low dim outline
of Long Island
through sunlit haze

overhead
a fat waning moon
hangs
in a blue sky

across the geography
i cast imaginary meridians
connecting myself
to the distant points
of a worldwide compass

REFLECTION

May 31, 1997

solitary egret
(reflection in the water)
picking his way
upcreek
wading
in the shallow part
along the bank
11 a.m.

the world
divides in two
upstream/downstream
egret & his reflection
right & left banks
the two ways
of looking
as i cross the bridge
over the creek

and turns back
into one ...
two banks
but one creek
two egrets
but one bird
two eyes
to one man
day & night
but one world

FEAR

May 31, 1997

Death is always lurking
                off the side of the road

drowning pond
freezing woods
burning house

it is always lurking
because
we dwell on it
& how
can we not
in the depths
of our fear & sorrow

until
we buckle up
our courage
& look across
the pond
with the fearless
eyes of love

MILL HOLLOW PARK
June 10, 1997
Fairfield, CT

black bog earth
of the carboniferous
mississippian ferns
in swampy woods
edges
of the lilypad pond
thick with life
wild iris flowers
in the grasses
along the underbrush
of the riverbank thickets

PELÉ

January 24, 1999

the cat
suddenly got sick
and died ...
ripped a big hole
in our family dwelling

quieter now ...
no more
slain animals
lying on the carpet
in the morning
no more
endless cries
for food
no more disputes
about feeding him

the hand of Death
always holds
the final card
but while life
roared through his being
Pelé lived
as much as anything
ever does
in this world

COLLECTION TWO

"The Dream of Love" and "City of Dreams"

THE DREAM OF LOVE

1. The Queen of Cups
2. Love in Exile
3. Variations on a Medieval Theme
4. The Countess of Tripoli
5. Letter to the Moon
6. End of a Dream

THE QUEEN OF CUPS

LOVE POEM

i was shot down
by the arrow of love
before i could make it
out of town
wounded in the heart
by a flaming smile
long dark hair
and the sound of my name
spoken in a soft
dusky voice ...
then the outbound train
sped me away
into the night
and now
the following day
still under the spell
of the sweet obsession
i run your picture
a thousand thousand times
through the camera obscura
of my mind

ALLEGORY OF LOVE

a large unpopulated field
allowed to run riot
one or more neglected graves
hidden in a far corner

across the way
the house of the heart
keeping watch
through the changing seasons

occasional wayfarers
straying through
are left unquestioned
this is a free land
wander where you will

SEQUEL TO A LOVE POEM

i saw my life
across a gulf
of frozen years
stray memories
drifting through labyrinths
of time
disappearing
around corners
of never-to-be-identified
worlds
irretrievable glimpses
of an existence
i am living
on the other side
of a dream
and am forever
unsuccessfully
longing to be in contact with

perhaps there is a day
i take your hand
and remember everything

THE SEARCH

immobilized
i like awake
in bed
waiting for a dream
about you

a thousand years
pass by
snow piles up
outside the cabin door . . .
i forget who i was

in the morning
the birds return
from the north
unable to locate
your whereabouts

i give them
a strand of your hair
and the color
of your eyes
and send them off
in new directions

THE DREAM

i am walking
with you
along railroad tracks
a few others
out ahead
going to some event . . .
youre telling me things
you dont like about me
why it cant work
then suddenly you dodge
under the tracks
trying to escape
and i follow
grabbing one of your legs
half buried in sandy gravel
begging you to stay
i awake

such a bad dream
is much better
than none

SEX

in pornographic darkness
the mind sinks
to the common level
dragged through thick lusts
in jungle dense night
of scrotal fires
tom-tom measures
of the blood
pounding in the café
of the bodys orgasm

all night long
in a tower
the alchemist
bent over distillations
& sublimations
cool star fires
penetrating
the garret window
hermaphroditic wholeness
of non-burning sulphur
married to the fixed water
of mercurial quicksilver

THE NAME

i grew up
in the fifties
on rock 'n' roll
there was
Mary Lou
Little Suzie
Teen Angel
& Angel Baby
Donna
Dianna
& Desireé
Valerie
& Florence
& all the others

i've listened to lovesongs
all my life
i'm reading the troubadours
to know my theme better
i'm ransacking the poetry
of the ages
for something to say

it's 1993
getting late in the game
this time
your name is girl
spelled
G   A   I   L

LOVE

is
this
secret
excitement
carried
night and day
in the heart
a new-risen plant
inwardly watered
in the soil
of the soul
a confidential
message
composed
by the self
in search of
the perfect other
a malady
an ecstasy
a delirium
tremens
crawling
in the dust
before the object
of its desire

Love's Despair

all day long
    snow falling
        outside the courtyard window

you are the absolutely beautiful being
    i was fooling myself about

THE MADNESS OF LOVE

i want to disappear
      for several years

      on the highways
      and in the small towns
      of the world

      writing love poems
      that get delivered
      through friends
      to you

meanwhile
in rags
hobo-like
hobbling down a road
gnawing the old bone
of your memory
until
in utter ascetic withdrawal
i write the poem
that wins your love

      and you come
      and rescue me
      from my wretchedness
or else
i am recalled
by your letter
begging me to return
and i arrive

resurfacing
in your arms
        with the secrets
        of the Holy Grail
        & the Philosophers Stone
        to give you
        for your love

'Dedicated to the One I Love'

i really think
the only thing
left to do
is to keep
falling
hopelessly
in love
never to know
the touch
of your hand
or the taste
of your mouth
or the feel
of your body
my body
in the arms
of the other
and to keep
writing
endless
hopeless
love lyrics
to you
or whoever else
is moving through
the single-file
passes
of the heart

'ALONE AND PALELY LOITERING'

hightide creek
running to the Sound
in the star cold night

i think i'll go back
to writing nature poems
sing by the waters
of Archeron
telling myself
all the tales
of old forgetfulness

Ruin and Realization

ten swords
pierce the prone body
lying face downwards
on the field
of subliminal consciousness
between darkness
& dawn

what i didn't want
to know
which the dream knew
perfectly well
has come true

i meant nothing
to you
at all

Requiem

down by the shore
the sea
wearing away
the foundations
of the world

passage of millennia

tide washing
over cold stone
in morning's blaze

when i knew you
it was 100,000 years ago

LOVE IN EXILE

MERLIN AT TINTAGIL

all alone
in the Tower of Love
a hermit's staff
to help him

         up
the crooked
      stoned
stairs

LANCELOT

many roads
wandering
directionless
in the house
of day
Sun
rules
and at night
Moon emblazoned
on a Shield of Darkness

Queen of Cups

you fall through
the mine shaft
of my mind
into a room
full of memories
exchanging places
with former occupants
mingling with the dust
of ages past
incorporated
into the woman
who is every woman
sitting enthroned
in the center
of the soul

Gawain

day and night
i ride
the high horse
of your memory
looking out
over the wide plain
of the earth
feeling
the cool breeze
of my uplifted thoughts

Tristan

there is only one
possible place
in the wide world
she could be
right now

perhaps
she is moving about
or else
at rest
gently breathing

he puts his ear
to the ground
and listens

Patronesses of Love

Aliénor of Aquitaine
Azalaïs
Bertraine
Rostangue
Phanette de Gentelme
Hermesende
Adalazie
Mabille
Stephanie
Jausserande
Ermengarde

AZALAÏS

```
                          of
              heavens          my
         the                       night
    through                          like
  move                                  the
you                                        moon


              u           a
              n           b
              t           s
              o           o
              u    &      l      radiant
              c           u
              h           t
              a           e
              b           l
              l           y
              e
```

PARSIVAL

out in the world
the vagaries of fortune
the slow turning
of an endless wheel
and man
riding alone
in the wonderment
of a childhood landscape
(in the youth of life)
encountering on the way
many symbolic forms of evil
in the guise
of knightly adversaries
and ever guided
by a vision of truth
embodied in the shape
of woman divine
shining like a star
in the high abodes
of castle walls

Galahad

a year
of fruitless wandering
shedding old rules
& habits
has not dimmed
your memory

i have finally
arrived
at the moment
that was meant
to be

in the hall
of the Fisher King
slowly
like dawn
replacing night
reality
entertains
its dream

Azalaïs des Baux

in the great city
where you are living
many castles
many streets
many thousands
many parks
& jostling fields
& gardens
many ships
many spices
many luxuries
from oriental lands
many beggars
many lepers
many ...

alone
in the country
of a dream
i am traveling
by a dark sea
the territories
of the world
spread beyond
the map of my mind
and i am looking through
the window of the soul
rain falling
in the windy night

VARIATIONS on a MEDIEVAL THEME

THE TROUBADOUR

every beautiful lady
needs a courtly lover
to sing her praises
and hope in vain
for her unattainable favors

i lost my stockings in the war
i'll have to sing to you
in this homely hobo's gown

The Lady

maybe
you were
queen esther
in a purim play
at school
and knew
from the beginning
what it was like
as an enchanted princess

or maybe
it came harder
in the deep struggles
of your life
by which you suffered
and fashioned
your beauty

lady esmeralda
queen of the night
the details
of your biography
are exceedingly speculative
i wish to know them
no better

that you have a biography
that there is an earthly counterpart
to your divinity
is what almost amazes me

CARCASSONNE

in the town
of thousands
& thousands
nevertheless
i keep thinking
i see you

would it be
the same
if i knew
you didn't live here?

The Lay of the Land

i am standing at the edge
of the stony continent
looking out
at you
living on the jewel of an island

i am living
in a cave
looking up
at you
in a castle

Phanette de Gentelme
tell me
how is your sister
Azalaïs de Porcairages?

and for that matter
how's Hermesende . . .
Asalazie
Rostangue
Mabille
Jausserande
and all the rest
of the old crew
high on love
in the rocky fortresses
of southern Provence

THE MOON

out on the highway
the blind leading the blind
no one seeing where to go
each tagging along behind
the other
lost & directionless

high-risen moon
of late afternoon
guide my steps
down the empty side road
back home
into the falling night

THE SEA

dogs barking in a mansion
i made my way
down to the level sea

the whole world
is trapped
in its plans
for the day

i'm the sidekick
of nature
wandering minstrel
of the naked shore

MEDIEVAL ITINERARY

from the East
the wealth
of Arab lands
Moslem civilization
throughout Spain
& Provence
drugs & spices
returning Crusaders
Jewish traders
on the pilgrimage roads
Hebrew scholars
in Toledo & Salamanca
Aristotle & the Greeks
moving west
Gothic Art
& Architecture
Latin Learning
Medieval Magic
Knights of the romances
cars of the tarot
hermits & saints
queens at the crossroads
of culture
teaching the arcane wisdom
of courtly love

Languedoc

romantic love
                    is a denial
of reality

                    a making perfect
of that
            which is not

it is a rebellious doctrine

                persecuted & exterminated
                along with the Cathar heresy
                by Pope & King

in the exotic
cross-cultural
lands
of southern France

Daydream

i come to that place
along the coast
where
when the tide's low
i can slip through
and continue around
the boulder-piled shoreline
to the eastern towns
and i pretend
youre with me
and we dash laughing
across the narrow inch
of dry-remaining strand
escaping the world
and entering
the remembered excitement
of an earlier existence

In the Still of the Night

in the cruel cold
of northern lands
scattered cloud
drifting through
moon-resplendent sky
in winter-silent night

Jaufré Rudel
the troubadour poet
(according to legend)
loved the Countess of Tripoli
whom he had never seen ...
he celebrated *Londhana*
—love from afar—
no joy
pleased him as much
as the enjoyment
of a distant love

the cruel cold
of the north
came down
wiping out the heresies
and the religion of love
carried by minstrel poets
retreated into Spain
& northern Italy
or in Germany
where it had been picked up

by the minnesingers
of the late 12th
and early 13th centuries

in the heart
there is a longing
in the heart
there is a longing
for a distant love

THE COUNTESS OF TRIPOLI

DISTANT LOVE

all night long
i lay awake & asleep
in a cold chamber
the moon outside
full and pale
and the great sea
separating Europe
& Africa
lies between us
like the distance
between masculine
& feminine
and seven years
have passed
& i have sung
your name
in the courts
of king & queen
and made
our non-existent love
famous
throughout the land

METAPHYSICAL THOUGHTS

the world is alchemy
and you are
the gauze-white moon
penetrating
thin
cold
cloud
haze

an ageless sea
an uninhabited world
the measureless distance
between
heaven & earth

b   s
o & o
d   u
y   l

separates us

in a castle
by the sea
i am looking out
at the void
enthralled

Jaufré Rudel

with a crusader's zeal
he took ship at Narbonne
for the Holy Land
(spiritual center of the world)
where the distant love
of his songs
lived
and he was dying
of love
took sick at sea
and was carried to an inn
in Tripoli
and she came down
from her castle
to his bed
and he revived enough
to tell her
that in her presence
he no longer feared death
and so he died
cradled in the immediate arms
of his distant love

AZALAÏS

wandering
in a forest
in France
I see your face
in the window
of a castle

you are dealing out
cards
in a dream

pentacles ... dazzle
swords ... go straight to the point
cups ... are the offerings of chance
wands ... are the fire that activates the world

TROUBADOUR SONG

i am in love
with someone
whose name
i do not know
and have suffered
the pangs
of jealousy
for someone
to whom
i've said
no more than
"hello ... how are you?"

i am acting
in an absurd manner
toward someone
whose gentle glance
or soft word
is sustenance
for a decade
and whose kiss
is immortality

The Return

many days
wandering
on the roads
through town
& city
& countryside
composing lovesongs
in praise of you
arriving finally
at Bordeaux
where you showed me
mercy
in a smile
& a greeting

fresh water
to wash away
salt tears

CHASTITY PROPOSAL

Countess
i hear you like to be alone
just like i do

perhaps we could live apart
and love together
in the burning waters
of a deep & distant love

REVELATION

there were always two

one was dark
one was fair

one lived in the city
one lived in the country

one was the moon
one was the sun

one was Valerie
one was Florence

one was Azalaïs
one was Hermesende

one was Gail
one was Mary Ann

both were   the Queen of Cups
                 &
                 the Countess of Tripoli

turned from door to door
i moved between the country
of two women
marrying them together
the dark & the fair
body & soul
silver & gold

moon & sun
uniting them in me
salt
sulphur
& quicksilver
we performed the alchemical magisterium

DISTANT LOVE (2)

i see you in a dream

you sit down
with a male friend
opposite end
of a table
from me
but seeing me
you get up & leave

out on the roads
of the world
i am wandering
a satchel of songs
tied to a stick

in the alleyways
of a dream
i turn & turn
lost in a maze of longing

Two of Pentacles

i moved between
two harbors
to the ebb & flow
of a tidal sea
between a port city
and a cove-hidden village
singing a song
of the Queen of Cups
in two of her manifestations
tossed between
the city of my birth
and the small town
of my wanderings

LETTER TO THE MOON

TRADE

on the roads
& through the passes
slow caravans
journeying from the East
pack trains
struggling over the Alps
Italian ships
sailing the inland sea
German vessels
hugging the Baltic coast
Swedish Vikings
floating products of the North
down Russian rivers
great faire
summer & fall
at Troyes Provins Langres
mingling the wares & peoples
of the world
small cars & drays
on the local roads
bearing the produce of the manor
songs of the troubadours
in praise of beautiful women
carried in the satchel of the mind
from castle to castle
by jongleurs & gleeman

LONELY WALK

dear Countess
the world is asleep
in the early hours
before dawn
i walk the road
down to the sea
cold cloud vapor
drifts through a prism
of shrouded moon
down to the waters
of a withdrawn sea
awakened geese
cry out &
fall back asleep

a n d   o u t   t h e r e
t h e   w i d e   w o r l d

in vast slumber
& stillness
absolutely absorbed
into the astral body
of its dream

AZALAÏS

rain   the mind's eye
snow   sees in the dark
sleet
hail

     fall   a land
                              where
                              the body
                              has not been

days
nights
weeks
months   in the castle
                              of the mind
                              pass by
                              i watch your image
                              dancing in a fire

in the Castle of Love
one constant remains

a wide smile on your face
light dancing in your eyes

Hopeless Love

the world
does not contain
the day
of our being together

a fantastic possibility
walks off
into eternity

again & again
like a fish
leaping out of water
i pursue you
in the phantasm
of a dream

Daybreak

All-seeing Sun

            blood gold red
            suffusing
            remnant cloud
            on low horizon

climbs out of the winter sea

            q
          u
        a
      r   Moon
        t
          e
            r

                half
                way   in transit

                back
                turned

                day
          rising
        the
    to

Queen of Cups

a deserted winter beach
midday sparkling sunlight

two elongated
skeleton shadows
thrown by the only passersby

tide at lowest ebb
gulls patrol the coast

measureless emptiness
of sea & sky

The Escape

in a dream
i am traveling westward
a thousand miles
to escape your memory

the cities change
the strangeness
of another life
envelops me
as i move beyond
the sphere of your influence

CHRÉTIEN DE TROYES

and the fields of France
were upon us
and we entered
the magical country
of romance
old legends
sifting down
from the mystical lands
of northern Celts
of a world
not wholly redeemed
from enchantment

LOVES OF THE TROUBADOURS

Agnes de Montluçon
Guillhaumone de Soliers
Rixende de Montauban
Azalaïs des Baux
Tricline Carbonelle
Procellette de Porcelet
Marguerite de Ries
Jausserande de Lunel
Huguette des Baux

"Beauty turns wisdom into folly …
I would be no coward if i turned
my eyes away from your beauty …
but when you speak I am unable to
leave your side …"

Peire Vidal to Azalaïs des Baux

Azalaïs

i am a beggar
standing on a roadside
watching you
walk down the path of life

i went up around
crossed over
doubled back
came from behind

and now
i'm standing on the side
of a road
looking at you
walk down the path
of your life

and i am throwing you
a flower
and writing you a poem
and acting ridiculous
and showing off

and you are passing me by
on the road of your life
over & over again
forever

END OF A DREAM

FANTASY

it's many years later
and you've returned
from sojourns across the sea
and from a marriage
and all the experience of life
and i am just a distant memory
long since forgotten
but a quirk of fate
(perhaps a poem i wrote you)
somehow brings us together
and all the possibilities
lost & found
come rushing back in
and this time ...

Outcast

in high disfavor
through palace gates
out city walls
onto the high road
through fields
of the countryside
forests of the landscape
i roam
gone from the dreamcastle
of your memory
like a wounded deer
stricken from your sight

Nine of Swords

in dark vaults
of the self

      hands covering the face
                collapsed
                in grief

    a voice
    wails & wails

        uncontrollably

a nightmare
awakens me

sharp swords
cut the strings
of my heart

DREAM'S END

from a long journey
into unreality
i am returning

the solid world remains
to take me back

nothing essential has changed

now
as i to you
so you to me
mean nothing at all

CITY OF DREAMS

Sketches of Albany (1)

enter over a bridge

dark waters
of the midnight river
swirl below

low-slung crescent moon
suspended over indistinct hills
to the west

fresh night wind
in the silent streets
blows the returning stranger
unnoticed
back to town

Sketches of Albany (2)

from within the structure
of houses on a hill
looking riverward
to daylight and distance ...
cool summer breeze
after the rain
combs the ivy mantling
on old grey masonry walls

Sketches of Albany (3)

i was walking with you
in downtown Albany
late one sunday afternoon
behind stately parapets
of the civic center
riverbluff-mounted
gazing eastward
for a clear camera view
of the Berkshires

young lords of the land
surveying their wide domain

Sketches of Albany (4)
State Street

long look of emptiness
down the endless street
of summer quiet

through shade trees
of the park edge
paled glow
of the shimmering
evening sun
rests on old brownstones stoops
and wrought-iron handrails

Sketches of Albany (5)
South Pearl Street

down from Respectable Hill
wild weedgrown backgardens
(wooden staircase, back porch and stoop)

dropping unseen
behind old brick housefronts
to 19th-century Hudson River
waterfront street
half boarded up and deserted

white-laced blue of the western sky
between gaps in the three-story building row

sun pouring down
on the ghost town streets
of the Old Port of Albany

SKETCHES OF ALBANY (6)
AMTRAK TRAIN

(Hudson to Albany)

river-inundated scraggly
brush-and-weed land
fronting thick and impenetrable woods

occasional
cobblestone-banked
drainage ditches
entering the forest
and meandering out of sight

old abandoned
squat depot buildings
wayside stations
railroad ties
crumbling or paint-weathered
frame houses

stately homes
lawn-surrounded
beside the two-lane road
paralleling the tracks

the margins and extensions of a wilderness
interrupted by houses, clearings and the road

Sketches of Albany (7)

and the summer moon
hangs in a vast sky
over Albany

over the bowl-like depression
of the ancient lake bed
now raised to riverbluff

nary a soul
in the amphitheater spaces
of the civic center
colossal public edifices
like modern obelisks & temples
rearing up in the ancient night

Sketches of Albany (8)

haunting your quiet streets
at night
tiptoeing
in the invisible world

(all albany asleep)

while i gaze up and down
the absolutely silent
house-filled avenues
of the unconscious mind

SKETCHES OF ALBANY (9)

(morning departure)

leaving behind
the open spread of city
rising up from the river
(quiet under fog-damp skies)
descending the brick-house streets
past ramparts of the civic center
past medieval church fortresses
downtown
to the bridge of loneliness
climbing above the river
in the pale-breaking light
of the journeying sun

CITY OF DREAMS
LOWER MANHATTAN LANDSCAPE

dusk
over the East River
below 14th street
the world
in fabulous grey intensity
bridgecable lights
strung between boroughs
gloom of the whaleback waters
running south
before a stiff breeze
warehouses
on the Brooklyn shore
low & silent
dotted by lonely lights
against a flattened landscape
receding toward the ultimate ocean

CITY OF DREAMS (1)

midnight
horse-drawn
carriage
alone
like a phantom from the past
in the fog-bound park

clip-clop
of the plodding horse
high
slow-turning
many-spoked
back wheels
lantern
swaying
above the buckboard

floating through the night
the accoutrements
embellishments
romance
& atmosphere
of a bygone era

City of Dreams (2)

two castles
(old waterworks buildings)
squat together
in a cove of the reservoir
shielded by tree of paradise woods

water laps gently
at the shins of stone walls
in the hot August sun

in the sealed
mysterious
interiors
of the castles
the debris
of abandoned alchemical experiments

CITY OF DREAMS (3)

in the dream
the night train
clatters through Long Island

impossibly connecting with Philadelphia
it never reaches New York

strange cars
from different eras
ride this line

on it
you never get where you're going
you lose your baggage
you have to retrace
through old
incredibly intricate
underground passageways

this is the country of dream
(outskirts of the outskirts)
you never wake up alive in

City of Dreams (4)

deep in the dark hours
after midnight
the sounds explode
off the city streets

bright moon
full of romance
floats overhead

all night long
the human world
pounds & throbs
till somewhere near dawn
i fall asleep
in the arms of the moon

Dawn

at the east-west portals
sun & moon
divide the world

yesterday has faded
and today does not exist

in between
the light
& the dark
the last dreams
of night
blaze up
in the fires of day

Addendum: Hudson River Ruins (1)

shallow clear-running water
in a narrow ditch
beside the tracks

cobblestone wall from a fairytale
(no one to see it)
embanking the higher ground

thickets of weeks and wildflowers
(Queen Anne's lace abounding)
thorny wild raspberry bushes

tracks and river
for miles
north and south

solid weight of the Palisades
to the west
looming up on the Jersey shore

sun blazing, wind blowing
in the pristine solitude
of high noon

(2)

no one

where
the rusted iron railroad bridge

(sections of sky between the rotted planking)

crosses high over the tracks

and drops
by rickety stairways

to the boulder-piled shoreline
of the ancient Hudson

(3)
YONKERS

first community north of the megalopolis
falls within the monster's baneful shadow

hodgepodge confusion
of old and dirty
new and ugly

worn-out
rapid-paced
urban exhaustion
where once

broad undulating slopes
old stone churches
quaint wooden houses
profusely-grown
picket-fenced
gardens

commanded wide vistas of the main river
and the farmland in the tributary valley

(4)

clouds are gone
and the sunlit moon floats supreme

nervous traffic
like rats scurrying frantically
never see the best part of the day

beside Lonely Wharf
dilapidated warehouses
(or maybe Pompeii)

windmills on Paulus Hook
and the Half Moon
now a Mississippi River steamboat
playing rhythm and blues
as we dance ecstatically
on the shoreline
of the dying day

(5)

wide sweep of the Harlem
under rocky Marble Hill

woods cleared for pasturage
on high surrounding banksides

empty platform of the railway station
(an outpost pacing America)

time poised eternally
on the high noon tracks
at the transition point
between country and city

(6)

castles of aristocracy
above river walls

forest-sheltered
rivulets
falling
shallow and rocky
to the Great River

old stone embankments
cluttered with wildflowers
along the water level
plebeian route
of the railroad

(7)

rains of the Cretaceous
and the red sun at dawn

half moon floating eastward
against time

mist rising from the river
as the first mammals appear
on the drenched earth

(8)

where the river
rank with sewage
sloshes in post-pier darkness
under warehouse shadow

you and i
out on the runway wharf
(old and ruinous)
gazing upon the openness
of river and sky

red sun
in a blaze of glory
dying over Jersey

large moon
full of romance
like alchemy
on the oily ripples
under the warehouse gloom

COLLECTION THREE

Yellow Sketch Book, 1995–2004

THE CAMDEN RIVERSHARKS
August, 2003

for a few days
when you play the home team
the box-score statistics
illuminate the darkness
and i get to see
who's in the lineup
and how each does

then you move on
playing someone else
and only the final score
is reported
in the newspaper
the rest left to the imagination

last time in Bridgeport
you swept the 3-game series
Maness homered twice
the second a 3-run jobbie
in the eighth
winning the third game
while Lipso Nava
went a respectable 3-for-11
driving in two runs
in the second game
playing a flawless third base

and so it goes . . .
the dust settles

and the heroes ride off
into the distance
the normal routine
is resumed
and only a final result
penetrates the overall
darkness of your doings

THE FROG
June 4, 1996

a day of continuous
(at times hard) rain
left the world so wet
that even a frog
was confused

up from the creek
out of the bushes
he leaped
flapping himself
in two great bounds
halfway across
a quiet back road
where he lay motionless
in the tunnel
under the overhead expressway

and i looked on
in horror
at the approaching car
hoping feebly
(hands held to my face)
to stop it
with a silent look of distress
(or else secretly, evilly
hoping for a direct hit)
while the car
hit it once
flipping it over

and i
who could have prevented it
but was too apathetic
to protest
watched
while the cold killer
that never saw a thing
had its way

GREENS FARMS

May 1, 1996

everything looks great
from the heart
of an open field
roll of the glacial land
at our feet
running off into distance
beyond farmstiles
made of old wooden rails
palely glinting
in cloud-whitened sunlight

GEORGE STREET

May 2, 1996

in the endless hours
of late afternoon
the children are playing
a wild game of keep away
on the front lawn
and the hot sun
of early may
alternates
with cumulonimbus clouds
and the soft zephyrs of spring
blow all day
for many days now
across the lawn
the children run
squeal and shout
on the safe-play
no-traffic
side street
and time lasts
all day long
in the morning sky
in the long days
of childhood

ALLEN'S CLAM AND LOBSTER HOUSE
May 23, 1996
(Westport, CT)

the lazy water
laps at the pier
the season
blazes towards summer
cooling breezes
bend the long grasses

out the picture window
long-distance view
across the tidal waters
of the mill pond
islands
spits of land
thoughts of the sea

the tables extend
down the long
galley-like room
wide berth
snug harbor
the framed light of day
looks in everywhere

thru wide glass windows
plays softly
on wood paneling
& tableware

all talk
drifts toward the sea
soft white flesh
of the brine
tasty on our palates
fresh bread & butter
& ale
to wash it down
while our eyes
feast thru the looking-glass
on the calm
inlet waters
of the sound

THE ARBORETUM
May 12, 1996

on the avenue
of landscaped estates
8.6 acres
remain for the public
as an arboretum

trees and vegetation
scattered thru a clearing
across a greensward
gently sloping
to the edges
of surrounding woods
we rest like lions
sprawled on the sunny grass
near tree shade
looking off into the distance
absorbed into the field
of our vision

CHINESE RESTAURANT
January 3, 1998

nothing much happening
during the off-hours
so the late-afternoon
card game
starts up
in the back

green tea
floats its jasmine fragrance
across cultural oceans
we embrace
the Chinese heart

up on the walls
sages wander
thru mountainous landscapes
into the monastery distance

DAY IN MANHATTAN
January 16, 1998

in the reckless city
in the underground maze
thru the high-vaulted passageways
of the art museum
down the snow-turned
rain-soaked streets
under the high-rise opulence
of the uptown
apartment buildings
past the elegant solidity
of brownstones
and the sorrowing poverty
of tenements
we turn and turn
in the birthplace
of my origins
thru the pinwheel fortunes
of our wanderings
in the great
amusement center
of the great metropolis
to be delivered
at last
to the station platform
of the grand central
transportation system
after the whirligig
of our unheralded
and unknown
adventures

SELF-PORTRAIT

August 29, 1996

i live like a hobo
camped along the railroad
riding the cars
up and down the line

in moonlit dreams
i wait for late-night trains
making their final run
from here into the past

i love the wide-open
prairie spaces
flatlands and marshes
and looking across fields

at night
i escape
to strange dark cities
called by familiar
daylight names

GREENS FARMS ACADEMY
July 15, 1996

i walk about the silent campus
and empty quadrangles
of the high school
grey morning in summer
nothing doing

buildings sit
waiting for occupants
school vans stand
in motionless rows
directional signposts
confront vacancy

the brick stone tudor buildings
make a van eyck painting
the courtyard
a setting for Shakespeare
the rolling campus
an Italian campagna
the wide private road
divided by
its grassy
tree-lined island
a French boulevard

all the European traditions
that come back again
in the fall

WALGREENS SHOPPING CENTER

July 18, 1996

old rusted crane
tilted against
blue summer sky

three men
on a rooftop
hauling something

cumulus clouds
work
above the scene

MAIN STREET TOWN

July 20, 1996

i saw
a man
come out
the side door
of his box-shaped
white-painted
house
and walk
down a
little
narrow
stone
path
between
cut squares
of lawn
behind
hedges
and pick
up his morning
newspaper
and return
up the path
and up the steps
to the white-painted
lintel
of the opening
door
into the shadow

of the entrance
in such
intensely
brilliant
sunlight
that the whole scene
became an abstract reality
a main town event
i could see
happening
back across
the years
of my past
to the first
days of school
and beyond

Allen's Clam and Lobster House

July 25, 1996

the lazy waters
lap at the pier
table conversations
repeat the endless clichés
grey daylight
and the broad expanse
of the cove
show beyond
big picture windows

the restaurant
becomes an aquarium
a boat
beached at dockside
and never sailing . . .
the sea looks in
thru the wide end
of the telescope
ducks dabble and preen
along the shore
or scoot about
the calm waters
in the lazy afternoon

seafood and ale
fresh rolls and butter
and the idle conversations
of casual talk
while we slowly surrender

to the opiated leisure
of the scenery
and the slow digestion
of the moment in time

SUMMER IN THE CITY
July 23, 1996

i saw the gypsy

READER ADVISOR
INDIA'S MOST GIFTED PSYCHIC

leaning in the doorway
of her street-level shop
2:30 p.m.
daylong
intermittent
rain

when i passed her
I looked for a sign
something occult
something magical
but instead
a commonplace yawn
was the only message

ALLEN'S CLAM AND LOBSTER HOUSE
August 14, 1996

the sunny Riviera
and the tideless Mediterranean
fade into
the historical distance
revealing the quiet landscape
of the Connecticut marshes
and the cove-indented shoreline
of Long Island Sound

seated beside great
picture windows
we are the observers
of the lost boundaries
of a drowned Eden
after the world-engulfing Flood

we drift seated
motionlessly rocked in place
taking a break from life
we watch the static portrait
of a post-diluvian emergence
thru the looking glass
in the shiphold
of the restaurant

NOMADISM

August 16, 1996

i was walking around
trying to be in
the empty spaces
of the picture
"hit 'em where they ain't"
"be where they wasn't"
not a total retreat
once and for all
but like the ecliptic
of the planets
cutting against the grain
not going around
in circles

LACEY PLACE

October 2, 1996
(Fairfield)

in day's sunlight
modern cement walks
official decorum
of company buildings
occupying
former junior high

parking lot
in back
fences out
the tracks ...
down an embankment
the river
under shadow
of the RR bridge

Comic Books
October 25, 1996

formed
our conception
of things
the streets and traffic
of Superman's city
(boasting a daily newspaper)
represented the national
small town metropolis
the woods
of Little Lulu's
imagination
when she spun her
didactic tales
to Alvin
(to hush his bawling)
was the forest primeval
of our collective unconscious
Archie and Veronica
Betty and Jughead
lived in nirvana suburbia
went to America's
small town highschool
and wore team letters
on their sweaters
Richie Rich
lived in the mansion
of our dreams
on rolling grounds
with swimming pools

and statues
Elmer Fudd
Bugs Bunny
and Yosemite Sam
taught us what
farmers' fields
rabbit patches
and desert sagebrush
were like
and though we learned
most of life
firsthand
the comic books
fed us
platonic conceptions
in three-dimensional
primary color
of our environment
and society

THE RETURN
November 15, 1996

i came back
from the big city
from the endless rush
to see
the ducks
in flotilla formation
gliding by the shore
in cold November waters
under blazing morning sunlight

the night heron
stood huge and solitary
a prehistoric bird
picking at the exposed mud
of the low-tide creekbed

down the beach road
(by-passed in November)
i went walking
saw the heron
saw the ducks
walked the beach
cleared my thoughts
and came back
to the world
carrying a clamshell
(two perfect halves
of a bivalve

still glued together)
as evidence
of where i'd been

SOUTHPORT HARBOR / EARLY MORNING
November 26, 1996

across the african plain
of the rivermouth
a dull yellow band
in the east
uplifting the sky

rowboats
tied to the wharf
bob gently
at low tide

atop strewn boulders
above the harbor's
marshy edge
i stand looking out

subdued shades
of yellow
pink
ochre and gray
unite heaven and earth

Greens Farms

December 6, 1996
(late afternoon, sky clearing)

i walk down
to the water
the great mystery
is flapping
at the coast
loneliness personified
i wander
deserted beaches

the sky is brazen
in the west
scrolls of cloud
like specters fleeing
like armies disbanding
roll out to sea
day's majestic conclusion
after snow and rain

gazing at the wasteland
of water
i lose track of humanity
the cry of gulls
is the only sound
and the motion of waves
mesmerizing the shore

New Year's Day

January 1, 1997

below the stone bridge
i saw the muskrat
swimming in the shining creek
burrowing at mid-day
in the low-tide rocks
amid the shallow returning waters

his vigorous little brown body
shook over its work
a creature in its own environment
out and about
in the warmest part of the day
before the water rose too high
before the sun lost its force

CHINESE RESTAURANT

January 14, 1997

hieroglyphic landscapes
on worn stoneware

divination pours
from an old metal teapot

we divide
our fortune cookie messages
into four categories:

advice
prophesies
parables
and character assessments

CHINESE RESTAURANT
January 14, 1997

table conversations
punctuate each other
scarcely intruding

uncurtained front window
frames
a winter-bright day

steam heat
warm tea
water chestnuts
and snow peas
like indoor opium
after Mongolian journeys

SWEET WILLIAM
January 19, 1997

johnny mathis' voice
croons thru the speaker
sweet love nonsense
oblivious to life's brutality ...
people in cardboard boxes
dying in new york
from winter cold
while we order crêpes
and hot mulled cider
served on flower-patterned
glass-topped tablecloths
sitting in someone's kitchen
amid pantry preserves
country antiques
paintings and mirrors
on the walls
everything tasteful
and elegantly natural

Morning/In Town

January 6, 1996

in the incredible perfection
of morning
i was walking
empty streets
past silent houses
in a blaze of sunlight
all the doors and windows
shut
to the truth
while i was climbing
uphill
into the continuation
of my life

THE ECLIPSE
September 22, 1996

over alpine woods
beyond a hillside
a lunar eclipse

rickety skeleton
of an old front porch
vine-entwined
in ghostly radiance
slowly advancing
shadow
slowly obliterates
memory
of earthly existence

EAST VILLAGE SCENE
January 20, 1998

in Yaffa's café
it's 1998
and Marvin Gaye
still bewails
the ecology
25 years later
in these times
that no longer
are changing

a winter's day
somewhere in between
light snow and sunshine
in the late
uneventful hours
of the afternoon
hot soup
with warm pita bread
goes down good

the East Village
survives and thrives ...
radical creativity
blooms
in basement cafés
and restaurants
in book and record shops
herb and healthfood stores

the years
have come and gone
like water
under the bridge
since Stevie Winwood sang
everybody knows the story
everybody knows the tune

SLEEP

February 9, 1998

lay
like a log
thru long
moonlit hours
having watched
the golden sun
depart in the west

daylight ambitions
held in abeyance
penetrate
crowd-filled dreams
thru memoryless avenues

immobile
in death dark
chambers of night
drugged by enchantment
prisoner of the moon
helpless in recalling
the trance-like
wanderings of the soul

PICKNEY PARK

February 11, 1998
(Rowayton)

brilliant sun
but the air
still cold
for our picnic
in the public park
beside the river

the greensward
slopes down
to the water
away from the road
and the hypnotic pace
of late-morning traffic
at the periphery
of awareness

we have our choice
among the scatter
of empty tables
and attached benches ...
free birds of passage
we alight briefly
in unrecorded moments
and then move on

MORNING ENCOUNTER
February 13, 1998

in dazzling
morning sunlight
the man
walking the beach
and i
exchange greetings
comment on the mild winter
wish each other well
and go our separate ways
warmed
by the brief contact
something of the ice
in my heart
starts to melt
each one of us
is a Robinson Crusoe
on his own island
looking out
at the wide empty sea

Chinese Restaurant

February 16, 1998

after we enter
the last lunchers
finish up
and the place is ours

Mr. Li
totals the takings
on the register
the cooks
take a break
resuming the eternal
card game
at the back table

no one else enters
a few orders
are prepared
for takeout ...
otherwise
the actors
have taken off
their masks
and the play awaits
its evening performance

CHINESE RESTAURANT
February 23, 1998

Mr Li
explains
the different
bean curds ...
light
chinese food
for heavy
american bodies

at the height
of the lunch hour
the restaurant fills
to near capacity ...
wheel of fortune
the business cycle
turns round ...

when the party
with the wailing baby
departs
table conversations
resolve
to a low hum ...
up in front
near the register
giant goldfish
dive
deep and strong

RAILWAY STATION
March 9, 1998
(Greens Farms)

the early morning
commuters
are gone
no train
for another hour
and the soul music station
plays to an empty room
while the overweight
black man
selling newspapers
coffee and donuts
takes a break
and heads for the bathroom

the morning rush
has spent itself
and the lull ensues ...
the wave has broken
against the shore
and in the aftermath
the soul music station
plays unheard
to a world
that's gone about its business

UNSCHEDULED VISIT TO THE
DARIEN HISTORICAL SOCIETY

September 11, 1996

hot middle
of a mid-week
before the end
of summer

not sure
if i have
the energy
or desire
to tour
the house

objects
with former uses
reconstruction
of a dead world

the value
of everything
appears later:
the perfect planlessness
by which we fall
into experience

DANDELIONS

April 22, 1998

parachute umbrellas
made of composite petals
lion-yellow sunwheels

the exquisite pain
of your being here
the indescribable pleasure

of spring
now that you're
thick in the meadow grass

Fairfield University

May 3, 1998

mist-enwrapped
and silent
in an atmosphere
of your own
above the town . . .
Jesuit sanctuary
of remnant woods
and retired walkways . . .
on your hillside retreat
i wander—
a library patron
too old
to go to school
one of the visiting
water fowl
congregated on the shore
of your unassuming duck pond

THE FIELD

May 27, 1988

behind the giant
video store
hidden from the main drag
a small field
overrun by weeds
bordered on three sides
by remnant woods
on the fourth
by the parking lot
and a row
of planted evergreens

sunlight's mellow haze
falls on the field
a light breeze
wafts lofty branches

cut off from use
here is the magician's
experimental ground ...
lying fallow
here is the restoration
of energy ...
nothing happening
here is pure potential
growing wild

SONG OF THE ROAD

September 14, 1995

the bridge is out
no cars
on Hillandale Road
while the heavy machinery
sits like an invading army
in the middle
of the afternoon

i come sauntering along
a free spirit
greeted by one of the workmen

i'm on the road of life
i don't have to make any detours

Sherwood Island

walking the plank
at the end
of the world
we cross
airfield strips
of flatness
approaching
the ultimate sea

strange alienated paradise
almost devoid of humans
now that summer's gone
the land returns
to its original lonesomeness

indians should be here
if anyone ...
white people
make no sense
with their lost pavilions
tree groves
and green lawns
amid these desert sands

alone
in brilliant sun and wind
we leave the park
on foot
by the main road ...

then down
the long steep embankment
to the RR tracks
and the shortcut home

THE MOON

December 8, 1995, 5:30 AM

full-orbed
thru bare trees
in cold night
the moon
holds the world
enthralled

i wander in ghostlight
under the enchantment
of far-off starlight
in the mystery of night

wandering moon . . .
i stand on the lonely road
in winding shadows
transfixed by the gaze
of your healing light

MORNING POEM

January 20, 1996

only patches of snow
remain
after the heavy rains
and though it freezes
overnight
strong red sun
in the morning
and the chirping of birds
bring the promise of warmth

the undaunted crow
caws loudly
in the woods
blending his cacophony
with the brave
warble and cheep
of two sweet-sounding birds

the sun glistens
on the frozen surface
of the marshes
the creek runs merrily
towards the sound
everything else is still
as i stand
on my hillside prospect
looking out
at the world at large

NOCTURNE

February 13, 1996

in lonely starlight

before dawn

waning moon

over fields

and black shadows

of bare-limbed trees

and the world

dreaming itself again

out of absolute actionlessness

erasing all memory

of yesterday

GREENS FARMS

March 20, 1996

i come up thru a gap
in the gate
into an old cow pasture
with a footworn path
leading to RR tracks
and an abandoned depot
with a pagoda-shaped roof

among woodchip piles
and neglected weeds
i eat my food . . .
the highway roars
in the background
sometimes deer stray
out of the woods
and thru a gap
in the scenery
i can see the creek
winding thru the marshes
out to the Sound

U.S. 1 / WESTPORT
March 27, 1996

black underbelly
of the wing-spread crow
coming to land
on the telephone pole

out of the imperious soup
in brilliant
mid-morning sunshine
the events of the Post Road
slow to a halt
at the traffic light

the rectangular spaces
of the shopping center
parking lots
frame the road ...
the crow
surveys the world
from his lookout
as i walk
into the hours
the fate of the day
now determined

THE ART EXHIBITION
(Fairfield)

snow falls
in late march
outside tall
second-story
windows

in bare empty rooms
on blank white walls
the paintings
await their viewers
flowers and vegetation
festoon the lower lobby
pretty hostesses
make us welcome
everyone comments
on the snow
a week into spring

in a big city
museums and art
on display everywhere ...
in a town
a scatter of paintings
once in a while
like a circus
or like an embarrassed moment
sidetracked
in the course of time

THE EMPTY BALLFIELD
April 18, 1998

perfect geometry
of a baseball diamond
from behind home plate

wide compass arms
of the foul lines
infield/outfield
remnants of an old
two-field
agricultural system
a nation
inventing a game

a small grandstand
directly behind the backstop
two wooden benches
(just enough room
for the opposing batsmen)
flanking the sides
of the steel-meshed cage

the field
looks far off
into distance
the road and highway
run in the background
the game that's not
being played
is being played

Exploration
April 26, 1996

tracing a creek north
unveiling submerged parts
of the geography
we come upon
a new development
slashed out of the wilderness
and climb a hill
up a road
past suburban homes
connected to nowhere

the light blue sky
of inland america
with soft cumulus clouds
looms beyond the hill
in the breathless distance
and down below
the creek runs
in the deep woods
thru stagnant swamps
choked with new-leafed briars
and fresh skunk cabbage

lost in the swamp woods
in the middle of day
we find an old horse trail
leading south
back to the main road
and the outskirts of civilization

CENTRAL PARK ZOO
May 1, 1996

in the tamed heart
of the metropolis
something wild
kept alive
snow monkeys
recalling asian rainforests
frolicsome seals
returning to sea caves
bears of the arctic
contemplating polar landscapes
calls of the wild
resound in jungle park
primitive sanctuary
in the cosmopolitan city
things that should not be here
captives of ocean and forest
set free in an imitation
of the night

BLIND PEW

March 19, 1999

like a dread summons
from hell
he appears
tap-tap-tapping
his blind man's
walking stick
down the cobblestones
of the sea-bordering road
a counterfeit
of helplessness
in the horribleness
of his maiming

the fury
of his demonic will
the hideousness
of his blindness
and tatters
make him
a more terrible commander
than either
Billy Bones
Long John
or Captain Flint

in his sightlessness
he is the incarnation
of night
in his poverty

the ugliness of want
in his cruelty
the pitilessness of fate
whom none will pity
when he thrashes out
wildly
in the road
calling on his companions
for help
before the horses
of night
ride him down

THE CONFEDERATE EXILES
November 18, 1998

seeking safety
in the land
of a former
national enemy—
nationless—
you found yourselves
unwanted

into the jaws
of a parallel conflict
beyond the world
of your understanding
you wandered
a far flung fragment
from the volcanic explosion
of a previous life

before the court
of a puppet king
your presented yourselves
ghostly veterans
of war
with no longer
a role to play
in the political
misfortunes
of the world

ATLANTIC LEAGUE BASEBALL

the big cities
don't even know
you exist
home team fans
taunt you
for not being
in the majors
national stardom
mocks the localness
of your endeavors

night falls
and in the equality
of the moment
comparisons fail
hierarchy is subverted
the provinces in revolt
the major cities
undermined
and the self-important
overlords
dethroned
by a servile population
of minor league peasantry

Harbor Yard Ballpark

July 10, 1998

we circulate
thru the empty upper tier
down the first-base side
feeling the evening breeze
watching the glaring sun
sinking in the west

shadows cover
the pitcher's mound
scoreless innings
follow one another
the evening grows cool

in the eighth
the Patriots
load the bases
scoring three runs
and the hapless Bears
once more
go down in defeat

before the ninth
is over
a bright orange moon
has risen
hanging above
the flattened skyline
like a giant baseball

THE ATLANTIC LEAGUE
July 2, 1998

now that
the inaugural season
is well underway
now that
word has gotten round
and people
can be heard saying:
"I went to a Bluefish game"
or
"I hear the Bluefish
have a real good team"
or
"I'd like to see a game"
now that
the ship of state
is successfully launched
and Bridgeport at least
is genuinely gratified
with its new acquisition
we feel like early pioneers
or gold-rush seekers
or like those who saw
towns spring up
out of the wilderness
we feel like those
who were there
when history
was still in the making

VIRGINIA LOVE

June 9, 1997
(Westport)

road
of suggestive
memory
sweeping uphill
in shadowed
sunlight
past foliage
and telephone poles
disappearing
out of sight
in a satisfying
question mark
of what's beyond

SOUTHPORT

June 20, 1997

Where a side road
begins to diverge
from the main drag
the abandoned restaurant
(closed for years)
sits—
a ruin in sunlight

in the shadow
of its decrepitude
tall grasses choke
the unused path
past broken front windows

at the edge
of the empty parking lot
weeds and short grasses
grow like house plants
over the crumbling bricks
of low bordering walls—
a desolate garden
beautiful in sunlight

NATIVE SANCTUARY / SUNDOWN

June 28, 1997

in the clearing
of the arboretum
the deer glides
thru evening stillness

the sun
still hasn't set
and the deer
moves thru
the transfixed world
not a blade of grass
stirring

the sun
is still glorious
in the treetops
as the deer moves
down the path
away from me
out of sight
back to the deeper woods

Erasmus

July 10, 1997

did you look
thru your window
at the european dawn
thru stone arches
like those
jan van eyck
used to paint
and was the world
real for you
as for us
or were you always
living in history?

The Bombay Restaurant

August 21, 1997

sitar
alternates with
tabla

irrelevant
ego-bound
table conversations
explode
in occasional guffaws

Indian waiters
come and go
exuding
perfect detachment

to the burnished glow
of subdued lighting
on white tablecloths
and rosewood furnishings
i am surrendering

to Indian culture
and Krishna
i am surrendering

to the spices
of the East
and the heavenly tastes
in the garden
of earthly delights
i am surrendering

Chinese Restaurant
September 3, 1997

hot afternoon sun
and windblown brilliance ...
the anonymous territory
behind the shopping center
the old chinaman
in soiled kitchen whites
is throwing the trash
into huge metal bins
and his action
irreducible in its simplicity
is happening
more than a thousand years ago

Chinese Restaurant
September 6, 1997

no customers
but us
in the in-between
hours
of late afternoon
the owner
and crew
occupy
the far back table
engaged in the daily mystery
of an oriental card game

we have wandered
into an old
charlie chan film
and these
are the authentic Chinese
practicing divinatory rights
in the guise
of a card game
spiritual enlightenment
in the magic lantern
of a restaurant

who are the chinese
so far from home
here in america
what is the meaning
of their journey
of the strange east
wandering in the wild west?

BRONSON ROAD
September 25, 1997

emerging
about mid-day
from old swamp woods
back of the river
crossing the stone bridge
on Sturges Road
we step beyond our limits
into new territory
discovering more ponds
on the other side
in more swampland

searching out
a new way home
we follow a road
we've never taken
past the everyday sight
of unfamiliar houses
and front lawns
past weeds and trees and grasses
around a bend
losing ourselves
without losing ourselves
straying homeward
thru forgotten country
of anonymous memory
wandering uncertainly
within recognizable parameters

Chinese Restaurant

September 30, 1997

we enter
leaving the sunny afternoon
on the other side
of the plate glass window
i direct my gaze
into the rainforest
of a fish tank

the last table
from lunch
finishes up
and the restaurant is ours

american rock 'n' roll
plays above
the museum stillness
of antiquity
we trade in the day
for the silence
of the years

CROWS

March 23, 1997

in the bright cold morning
the crows
dominate the world
outcawing the songbirds
commandeering the treetops
sending messengers abroad

chatterboxes on high
lawless adventurers
exultant in their freedom
theirs is the response
above all others
speaking back at Creation

FAIRFIELD SHOE SALON

November 7, 1997

elegant shoes
on display
the height
of european fashion
small town
main street
store window

untouchable grace
of the feminine form
simulated in polished leather
instep curves
and tapered high heels
enough to make
any man
a foot fetishist

cigarette dangling from mouth
one eye asquint
the small hunched frame
of the proprietor
(a dry and wizened
Frenchman or Italian)
leans on the counter
in afternoon boredom
without worry

he knows his shoes
are irresistible
there'll always be someone
to pay the price
for high-class merchandise

CHINESE RESTAURANT

November 21, 1997

the giant goldfish
dive
to rainbow depths
red lantern light
suffuses
the long rectangular room
burgundy napkins
lie folded
on white tablecloths ...
outside
the dull afternoon
turns to evening grey
Chinese
is exotic
but controlled
simple
but ceremonious
open-faced
but impenetrable

SOUTHPORT
March 10, 1998

dog barking
off in the distance . . .
i walk
under the tracks
wet tunnel
dripping in bright sunshine
after the snow . . .
up the path i go
past the railway platform
on the other side
into the high noon
of a western movie

THE BRIDGEPORT BLUEFISH

June 29, 1998

the local heroes
are gone
to Atlantic City
and Sandcastle Stadium

ocean waves
pound the Jersey shore . . .
old boardwalk
gambling
people living by the sea

back in Bridgeport
at Harbor Yard Ballpark
perhaps a lone groundskeeper
is raking the soil
of the pitcher's mound
in the empty house of cheers
recovering from recent excitement

Thanksgiving Day

November 27, 1997

Thanksgiving
as a kid
meant getting out
of the city
for a day
going to a big
suburban house
on Long Island
to be with family
in the warm cocoon
of belonging
sheltered from
the anonymous indifference
of the cold world

excitement at seeing
all the relatives
the big table
with the delicious dishes
made by aunts and cousins

the long meal
(central event of the day)
so much to choose from
and the deeply satisfying
repletion at the end
the women
cleaning up
in the kitchen

and the menfolk
offering token assistance
before retiring
to the living room
to loll before the TV
and repeat more
of the truisms
of yesteryear

Thanksgiving, 1997
i walk down
to the beach
in the early morning
the wind is blowing
after last night's rain
the sun is rising
i shed a few thoughts
on the pilgrim fathers
but i have no real reverence
as i reach the shore
and set off into
just another day

THE SALT MARSHES
December 2, 1997

first ground
reclaimed from the sea
ordovician ooze
primeval mud
acres of waterlogged pasture
thick with cowlick swirls
of salt hay grass
(marsh elder bushes
at high-tide edges)
carved by creeks
level with the horizon

habitat
of heron and egret
fiddler crab and bivalve
muskrat and beaver
deer and raccoon
swan and duck
osprey and seagull
marsh rosemary
and glass wort
spartina grass
and false indigo

lonely
irreclaimable
alternately flooded
and drained
devoid of human activity

subject to the rhythms
of the sea
antecedent and inhospitable
to man

BOMBAY TAKEOUT
December 5, 1997

the coke machine
hums in the corner
token decorations
cover otherwise
bare walls
local-events newspapers
rest on their metal stand
a few potted plants
of a single variety
six or seven small tables
each seating two
packaged goods from India
lining makeshift shelves
in a simple
adequate-sized room
the kitchen
half-visible
in the back

all the essentials
the minimum requirements
without embellishment
the food served
on plastic trays
in disposable containers
no one else
in the restaurant
while we feast regally
in a quiet chamber
of the commonplace

In Search of the Miraculous
December 28, 1997

i bought a set
of rubber farm animals
a kid's toy
at the local hardware store
set them up
on a table
at home
they reminded me
of the manger scene
it was the day
before Christmas

on the following day
passing by the area's
last remaining farmstead
i saw all the animals
standing stock still
on the corralled hillslope
looking at me
living representatives
of those
i had placed
on the table

something moves
behind the scenes
like in a chess game . . .
the pieces are played
and the world
comes into being

CHINESE RESTAURANT
December 31, 1997

on a Chinese screen
a woman's pavilion
floating palace
on a lake
the lady
at her table
entertained
by musicians
and dancers
other members
of her retinue
at various activities
in the surrounding area

black lacquer
white ivory
green jade

in the background
a small pagoda-roofed
structure
half hidden
by foliage
recedes
into the background
of the jungle night

HARBOR YARD BALLPARK
June 23, 1998

monster factories
belch white smoke
into evening skies
prayer-offerings
of an industrial city

monolithic stanchions
of a future highway
rear ominously
like a modern Stonehenge

beyond the centerfield fence
the wide spaces of America
extend into the distance

Metro North's
special train
offering personalized service
to the handful
of aftergame travelers
overlooks the action
as night falls
beyond the brilliance
of the high powered floodlights

Chinese Restaurant

January 2, 1997

opium and the buddha
come from India
the Japanese islands
lie out at sea
mountainous Korea
is swathed in mystery
the barbarians
grow restless
beyond the great wall
the foreign devils
come from across
the ocean

china lies
at the heart
of civilization
man-apes
lived here
before the dawn
of man

in the room
the ancient tastes
and aromas
circulate
china is old
china is
from the beginning
china is
the inscrutable past

MONDO PONDS / MILFORD

April 23, 2001

a steady breeze
fans the ponds
sunlight pours
unstintingly
on late-April bloom

recent debauches
are revealed
in scattered patches
of broken glass
while we wander
pine-needle paths
in the shade
of protective forest

chain of five ponds
(once gravel pits)
interconnected
by miniature waterfalls
a man-made
nature-made system
unfolding progressively
from small pond to large
before the delighted eye

New Haven

July 27, 2001

diagonal paths
cross the green
church bells
mark the quarter-hours
i sit on a bench
incongruously reading
a paperback western
under a hot
mid-morning
summer sun

the Spanish man
sitting on an adjacent bench
leisurely feeding the pigeons
is soon joined
by two cronies ...
they sit and smoke and talk
commenting on the birds

traffic moves
at the edges
the daily business
of the world
gets done ...
but here
in the time-stopped world
of the green
men with nothing to do
mark the hours

like the church bells
and life proceeds
without intention
to the slow motion changes
of the inert will

SOUTH PINE CREEK BEACH
September 25, 2001
(Fairfield)

pirate cove
perhaps . . .
up against
the vine-clad
earth-bluff
maybe they careened
their ships
and surveyed the sound
thru spyglasses

mid-day waters
swell toward the shore
no boats at sea
we gaze along the horseshoe curves
of the indented coastline
out to the point at Norwalk

they left their spirit here
click of coin
and the rough jargon
of another age
then sailed away
into eternity

SOUTHPORT HARBOR
February 24, 1997

the moon hangs
over the pre-dawn town

shells of low-tide
lie in mud and sand

unbegun day
lies poised
behind the hill
before creation

universal calm
enthralls the world
the incoming waters
return with the dawn

EVENING MEDITATION

February 27, 1997

how long's it been
since i've really
seen the sky
the slow drift
of diaphanous cloud
below the higher
rorschach patterns
and the patternless
gunshot realms
of pure chance
aglow in the west
hiding a setting sun?

NOSTALGIA
August 27, 1996

i watched the boys
playing together
on the beach
at the water's edge
finding shells
and other treasures
skimming stones
swimming
and talking
in funny voices
having a good time
in general
absorbed in their activities
yet still aware of me
(or so i thought)
flattered at being
an unsolicited audience
i gave them my attention
looked across the years
from forty-eight to ten
and wondered
what it felt like
at that age
tried to remember
and even thought i did
for a second
while the seagulls ran
and cried
at the edges of the tide

and the sun changed
from hazy to bright
to hazy again
and spread its warmth
deep into the soft sand
i looked on
with that mixture
of envy and superiority
an adult feels for youth
watching these two lives
dance in the sun
content to be myself
though wishing
i could know
once more
what it's like
to enjoy life
and the world
at ten years old

FAIRFIELD

March 5, 1997
(the playground)

at noon
the town
still slumbers
in grey mist

redwing blackbirds
and crows
out on the marshes
call to a hesitant sun

the day
takes its time
like a woman
at her dressing

no breeze
rocks the cradle
nothing stirs
humpty-dumpty
from the perfect balance
of his precarious perch

Harbor Yard Ballpark

November 13, 2003

the field basks
in naked splendor
under November skies

no groundskeeper
attends to the puddle
near first base

resting from overexcitement
the field lies fallow
repairing itself
in the silence
of the off-season

THE BRIDGEPORT BLUEFISH
September 22, 2003

all season long
victory & defeat
in all its forms
up until the last
ultimate game
to decide the winner
of the divisional playoffs

in the high
holy domain
of the dark Tower
having mounted
the stairs to victory
(one strike away)
the lightning flashed
and in utter bewilderment
you tumbled to defeat

now the horses come
to pick up the pieces
but you remain
on the field of play
absolutely stunned
while the whole
inexpressible meaning
of the long road
you've traveled
descends upon you

Board Games

we're all
moving our piece
on the gameboard
of life
(so to speak)
coming to places
we have to turn around
& go back
or remain
through several throws
of the dice
or possibly advance
in one quantum leap
& bound
and there are those places
we re-pass
again and again
like the familiar streets
of a town
or the prominent landmarks
of the natural terrain
and there are messages
& pronouncements
awaiting us
like the dictates of Fate
and rewards
and penalties
and opportunities
and it's all so much
like the real thing

except more clear-cut
& simplified
& made into a game

WORDLESS ENCOUNTER

high winds
& the dazzling
afternoon sunlight
of an april 5th
nor'easter
cold enough to snow
but brilliantly bright
in the parking lot
of the elementary school's
futuristic world . . .
carrying his schoolbag
he turns
to look back
at me
(looking at him)
sees something alien
& free
catch his attention

HARBOR YARD BALLPARK

(View from a passing train)

first the long emptiness
of the parking lot
then the stadium
low & fort-like
circular & rectangular
then the yellow dirt
of the infield
like Saharan desert sands
under mild blue skies
in early May

SASCO CREEK
April 16, 2004

every Spring
i come out
onto the marshes
and observe
the old dead-limbed
solitary tree
(limbs like a candelabra)
still standing
on the peninsular bank
of the creek
where the swans
have their breeding place

sometimes marsh birds
perch on it
like omens ...
it points upward
in crooked directions
and looks lightning-struck
a bare skeleton
oblivious to time
standing as an eerie monument
to itself

PORT CHESTER

backs
    of
houses
     at
       irregular
    angles

untidy
backwards
    sloping
      down
        to
         the
          river
  slanting
 early morning
april sunlight
     (as i ride by
     on the speeding train

"Miscellaneous Poems"

REPORT TO THE AUDUBON SOCIETY

they like old dead trees
upon which they drape their blackness
and with their cawing
they shake the branches

when leaving
they don't reach for the sky
but drop
great-winged
over the earth

they do not like roads
because by nature
they share no kinship
with the straight and narrow

their cry is harsh and jagged
and they speak to that cut
in time
called death

Leaving Colorado

<pre>
              water
              sluiced
                    thru the
         newly
                   erected
              house frames
                        runs un
       der the pine
                 boards
                    and finds its
way
     down
             hill
                into
                     town
</pre>

          gravel mud red clay earth
          in heaps
          like ignitible powder

               broken rock stone & clay
               where the floors will be

the sun burns behind tall pines
on the slopes of broad foothills
that swell towards the west

          the loose remains of the day
          get pocketed
          it becomes colder
          different trucks start up

the crackle of workmen's laughter
is a sound
dying on the hillside
into memory

Dreams of the West

they lived an incredible immensity
and sat for hours
in dimly-lit backrooms
drinking whiskey
and playing an esoteric form
of the tarot
(adapted to frontier conditions)
with only some wooden boards
separating them
from the wildness
they were a part of

They lived in the total revelation
of the continental magnitude
the memory-obliterating newness
of an inconceivable spaciousness
drinking deeply of the elixir
of immensity
(like the cowboy
who they sometimes were
and the horseback Indian)
grew to legendary proportions
in a legendary land

The James Gang

land of farms
back roads
and ways out of town

Russellville
Kearney
Gallatin
Corydon

rivers to be forded
hidden caves
and mineral springs
back up in the hills

railroad tracks
posse on the trail
separate and rendezvous
alibis and denials
to the newspapers
shadows of masked men
in the moonlight

Quantrill's raiders ride again

MANHATTAN

(In the times of Captain Kidd)

At night
someone lugging a chest
upstairs

by day
sun spread
on squared fields
of Indian corn

pieces of eight
reales & pistolas
coin of the realm
sun's rays
and kings' crowns
on fire-forged metal

over bramble-topped hills
through the swell
of meadow & dale
noiseless Indians
treading the wampum trails

THE ANTIQUES COLLECTOR

(after a painting by Carl Spitzweg)

shadowed stone stairway
leading up from the hovel
of an underground shop

glimpse of blue sky
and the topmost towers
of a European city

Two society women
ascending the stairway
gab over new-bought purchases

One leg bent over the other
book held close to the face
low-brimmed cap
over bespectacled
crag-worn features

The antiques collector
sits amid the ramshackle
environs of his trade
eyes turned up from his book
catching the viewer's glance

April

Maybe she travels in an english coach
along a cinder path
crossing a wooden bridge
and along the path
are many great-limbed trees

The color she brings is apricot
and her sun is a diamond
flowers appear on her way

I don't know if she is a beautiful
slip of a girl
or a plump queen
a mixture of majesty and pettiness

In her are rain and love
and the blossom
and from the back of the coach
she hums a distracted air
"April, appear, I will"

ALCHEMY

And a stranger
came in the night
to the house
of the disbelieving chemist Helvetius
carrying in a handkerchief
two pieces of the Stone
but refusing to reveal their secret
until again
he came in the night
finally granting the chemist
the smallest portion
of the wondrous substance

(when Helvetius, thinking it not enough, asked for
more, the stranger broke what he had given in two,
then threw one half away, claiming that what
remained was still more than enough to perform
the transmutation)

promising to return
the stranger never did
and Helvetius
at the urging of his wife
experimented on some lead
bringing forth the most perfect gold

THE GRAIL LEGEND

There is a king
who is old
who is injured
who has been slain
and he waits
for a redeemer
on an island
in the sea
or in a castle
by a river
impassable like the sea

And this is the sad-faced
realm of the dead
for death is an enchantment
a stealing away
of the soul
which lives on
in a magnificent castle
in the midst of
the wide wasteland sea
a splendid hall
with miraculous relics
and magical plenty

and it is because
the veil of wonder
has been lifted
from our eyes
and that we have lost faith

that we fail to see
this world
and why it remains
a wasteland

REPORT FROM A HEATH

They're coal-black
and they fly in troops
and communicate with each other
and there is a mystery
about the intensity of their doings

if they were human
you would say of them
they spoke a primitive gutteral tongue
and belonged to a region & culture
bordering on the blasted & blasphemous

They know no rules
and against a pure-blue autumn sky
their blackness has such a vibrancy
you would think it a color or cloak
they had captured for themselves

They appear friendless
like vagabond lords
whom the world will have no truck with
and in their sovereign isolation
they seem to have been bequeathed
the realms of distance & space

and if they cry out
from pain or joy
at their homelessness
that yakking seems only a defiance
proclaiming a further uniqueness

THE BLUE PARROT CAFÉ

in everybody's past
a blue parrot café

above the mantelpiece
in porcelain glaze
sits the totem bird of sailors
bedecked in gaudy jungle hues
dispelling the raven's solemn gloom

down the street
of some inland city
he sits behind a window
wearing the colors of paradise
magic of islands
on the dusty shelves
of the backroads world

DREAMS OF THE WEST

somewhere
buried alive
in the depths
of my past
the Montana kid
fights on ...
in the gulch
the western sun
is slanting
alkali dust
lies thick
on the plains
and high up
in the windings
of the canyon
old weathered boards
of the mining shack
warp and sag

OLD ENGLISH

language
out of
the dark ages
runes
carved
cryptically
blood-ash
spell chant
alder tree
rowan tree
hazel tree
boreal mesolithic
land of wotan
whale's way
swan's road
frisia
the elbe
metal clanking
on stone
jewel brooch
on handwoven garments
centuries
passing
in the dark
moments
of a dream

VIEW FROM A TRAIN

down an angle of deserted street
I catch a glimpse
of the absolute quiet
of the undisturbed night
the warehouse-empty
edge-of-town stillness
of an immaculate inactivity
hallowed by the ghostly illumination
of a solitary streetlamp

TRAIN STATION/JOHNSTOWN, PA

Weathered brick warehouse façade

rusted antiquated carloads
of wide-hooped iron cylinders
sitting forlornly on a sidetrack
in chill sun & shadow afternoon

graveheap of the iron and industrial age
in a northern mountain town

ALCHEMICAL POEMS (1)

another day
is dawning
in back of
the day

you remember
that which is
to come
the natural order
reestablishes itself
in a dream

ALCHEMICAL POEMS (3)

the sea in a dream

twilit obscurity
of the unconscious

all known landmarks
obliterated

gingerly
I step ankle deep
in the waters
of a higher
than natural
tide

GRAND CENTRAL

most of us
perhaps
are sitting
in a railway station
with nothing
particular
to do
in the perfect
dislocation
of Saturday night
half-sad
half-contented
half-listening
to some
sentimental Jazz band
and the slow passage
of time
unimpatiently
waiting
for the next train
to take us
into tomorrow

NIGHTSCAPE

out in the distance
I hear the low growl
of the ebb-tide sea

an hour before dawn
the moon rests
on the western horizon

nothing happening
only the constant murmur
of the sea
the eternal stars
and the slow passage of time

BASEBALL CARD MEDITATIONS

1.

He takes his hand out of the glove and smells the rawhide. Reading the book on Indians, he imagines a common blue sky of smoking clouds over the great boiling kettles of the village and the long poles of the tipi. Someone is always surrounding the tipi on his way to get in. There are discarded rock chips and broken spoons the archaeologists of silence are waiting for, the hill returning over the village. There is a road that leads invisibly across the village and visibly into the woods on both sides. In that western place where the sunny continuum of the rocky plane is broken continually by groves of shade-giving trees and we watched Robin Hood western outlaws on TV waiting for and chasing each other. This is the place in the city where we rode our glassy bikes on the cement roads of mercury with a vision of flowers stuck in the top of our heads. If we concentrate only on the flowers, we are in the forest of the names of flowers, the geometrical heads being thrust in our heads out from a black tapestry of what must be vertical soil in order to give us the true names of themselves from an explosion of shape. There is always a black and color combination that collects itself around the top part of our bodies. Around our bellies a shade swells formed by the bent trunk of the circular village. Around our hearts, though a grey mercurial rain is constant, the three of wands with its gathered clouds descends on the red shape of the heart. It is in this region that we have no voice, that they come from Hawaii onto the mainland and find that the distance goes up and stops and drops right down across the end of the plumb-line length of their arms. It is the place in which Little Lulu told the stories to Alvin, how the poor little girl with patched-up red dress went out to pick berries in the forest: a soft rain was forming, a soft loss of direction was growing as Lulu told the projected dream of her own self, actually told to Alvin the great secret of all our dreams and stories, which is that we have no voice in them. This image of Lulu walked dumb and poverty-stricken in the great simple forest with the great telling rain and could not speak a word while she gathered information berries and met the daughter of the witch-heart of the forest. Their voice goes up and comes right down, they are the dumb cows in the near field of the island, all their actions turned to meaning, all their works broken in the grey elements of the stone and the grey flowing principle of mercury. We are on the floating islands of Perelandra, moving away with the sun under our tongues, just the way Ted Lepcio, former second-baseman for the Boston Red Sox in the fifties, came out of the great blue background of the dream and rode in on the sunny morning where I found him sitting on my bed as I tried to fill in the rest of the Red Sox infield only to realize that the names have gone past us, our mouths form to say them and they are not on the tips of our tongues, what is are the gestures and materialities that we remember them for, like their secret mineral strengths, as the first-baseman of the fifties whom I couldn't remember, who played in the Boston infield with Lepcio and all I could see was a figure in a white circle of light (this from the card) and the fixed bat on his shoulders and now the game comes back, it was Dick Gernert but even his name has gone into mineral, it is the garnet, it is the buried earth. We do move along a mineral current moving under the earth, the strengths and weaknesses of the players are the outcropping rocks from which we later plumb the depths of the deep blue sea green of earth. They come from the exotic vegetation of Hawaii and are hitchhiking across the sand fields of Colorado but at their feet are the rare earth minerals of that floating magic-carpet tract of earth and in their eyes are the projected manual ends of their bodies and across their hearts they are struck dumb with joy.

2.

The names are in the clouds: Chico Carrasquel fields white baseballs as a shortstop in heaven. The bleached wood of the houses on a street of houses under the heading of sun: he talked about what major-league baseball was like in Cincinnati because this was Chicago and Comiskey Park we were heading for down the white streets and it could have been Cincinnati for all I know of the two cities—the knowledge that Cincinnati's ballpark doesn't hold much over 30,000 people and this was a small section of town, a residence we see through walking here, people who live here dream through to wherever they go, trapped in a greater metropolis in the subway in the dream or walk right out of the town from here. He talked about Cincinnati's ballpark and while he did I dreamed the figure of 30,000 as we walked the street. These are temporary houses, this is a temporary house for the ballpark in Cincinnati, his nostalgia for the city reaching back across the morning and his plan to come to the game with us. This is one thing on another: we project metals out through what we have known them as. Totally different from when I remember the games I've seen on TV of the Mets playing at Cincinnati, the announcer saying that only Willie Stargell hit one in that part of the park and what is this city where the end of the outfield slopes upward and there are all sorts of rulings for balls hit above and under a certain line, this Ohioan backwash city sitting like its stadium on the idyllic cast-off dream of the river, a city that threatens on another geological zone, the hillier West Virginia and that culture.

3.

Jerry Walker: Orioles, the year that had blue and white stripes on the rookie cards. Arnie Portacarrero: a name trapped in blue, how we are doomed to a career under the sky; behind them a fire of arms winds abstractly in cloudy blue space. There is a heavenly vision of the ballplayers worked by the medium of the cards. These days: gas stations and the sea gulls of gas octane over the river and the vision in sunlight, the imagined garden where there was none and the baseball cards get flipped out of our windows while the vision of the triboro bridge still works metallically like sea water in the back of our heads. Flipped out of the windows where they float in the windy sunny air as opposed to cards we have in our heads that show a specific cumulative perspective on the quiet church outside the window on a rainy day when no one is walking the streets, down under them where it continues to rain on the other side via the cards. We actually walked in the grey alleys whose insides are caused to exist by the outsides of the equally grey buildings, one thing throwing the other into relief. We send the cards out as messengers to bring back what is different from the fixed spatial distance of sea and bridge and avenue. We rose up, my father got up enough energy for going out in the park and playing the game of baseball in our territory.

i pretty much
dropped out
of professional baseball
as far as following it
goes
after Mickey Mantle retired
but i hung on
for a few years
with the Houston Astros
& Jim Bouton
picking up the games
at night
in Boulder Colorado
on a faint radio station
hoping they might need him
in relief

baseball cards
were my first tarot deck
i bought & traded
& flipped them
all heads or tails
matching
i remember names sometimes
Del Rice
Milt Bolling
Arnie Portacarrero
Johnny Klippstein
like magical formulae
alive with secret meaning

it's all over now
has been
for a long time
my life got crazy
in the '70s
marijuana took away
my innocence
i turn around
to look back sometimes
but i know
i can't go home again

"80 Sheets" Notebook

THE QUEEN OF SOUTHPORT

five streets
asymmetrical arms
of the starfish
radiate & converge
at a common center

queen of cups
gazing in a magic chalice
tossed on the tides
of the sea
in your sorrow
what do you dream
in your sweetness
who do you love

sailing into your harbor
all was quiet
tree-shaded lanes
picket fences
houses of the gentry

in a castle window
i saw you standing
looking out
over your domain
quiet smile
was on your face
trace of tears
in your gentle eyes

THE SANDBOX

the littlest ones
climb up the sides
of the world
and perch there precariously
clinging like new-born bees
to the world's vine
before falling back
into the sun-filled matrix again

these fledgling ducks
crawl upon their own shadows
and in their struggling
seems to signify
an eternal rising & falling of man
from the pit back into it

some carry off sand in sieved spoons
only to return to their starting places
sandless again
thereby enacting underworld punishments
they never feel the pain of

their mothers sit enthroned
around the rim of the pit
and the trunks of their legs
reach down to the sand below
like solid trees
or marble pillars
of an edifice
built in the minds of children

the sun bakes a cake of sand
in the cool late afternoon
of a spring that came today
and the older children
lay out new tiers of sand
atop the hardened sides of the pit
using shovel and pail

and there in the swarm
of sunned beings
in the sandbox
among the different age levels
that play & wallow & wonder
open-eyed
and cast-eyed
and excited-eyed
i glimpsed beginnings
of mesopotamian cities
earthworks of babel
and other many-tiered experiments
in the childhood of man

To Tom Hughes

4/5/01

the anonymous club
of elderly men
who make sure
the trains are on time
each maintaining
a lone outpost
at the edge
of his property
a silent vigil
confirming the routines
of the adventuring world
in its flight
between unknown distances

Rock Hill

scattered settlements
on a mountaintop
no idea
where the rest of the world is
i walk down the vacant road
of late afternoon
strange to be anywhere
but especially here
lost in a giant's fairytale

REJECTION

now the river's
at lowest ebb
only the merest trickle
of channel water
meanders
over the puddled surface
of exposed mudflat bottom

overhead the sky's
hazy grey
chance of rain
soft breeze
ruffles the june foliage

at the gates
of your kingdom
ten thousand words
lie shattered
on a barren plain

i'm the scavenger
of my own battlefield
picking up the pieces
to fashion you
another hopeless lovesong

LOVE POEM

your hair was pale gold ...
you woke out of dream
in the bed of the Three Bears
you were Cinderella
sweeping up a general store
the stories you heard
you were the heroine of
girl in the corner unnoticed
girl in the ashes
cinder girl

someone bought you a stuffed animal
you smiled
you had a mother
you swam in a lake
you saw the sky
you felt the rain the cold
the dead of night
you went to school
you had daily routines
(sometimes incredible experiences)
you thought of boys kissing you
you lived in a town
you visited the city
you had relatives
one summer you traveled
you hurt yourself once
you were sick
you had a father
a brother

an older sister
the first boy who ever ...

tell me
queen of cups
all the things
that have been you
tell me
over & over again
the life you've lived

Love Poem

you lived
in a house
on a street
in a town
& one day
something happened
& the world
was no longer
the same
& this was growing up
& you knew

all the dreams you had
drifting thru long afternoons
faded into evening's
setting sun ...
a chill wind
blowing across the land

you felt your aloneness
you were a girl
living in the world
going to school
you had parents
family & friends
your name was mary ann

tell me
queen of cups
all the steps

in your development
tell me
over & over again
how it's been
being you

After the Summer

now the light is perfect
falling through the length
of sad october afternoons
warm & healing &
absolutely radiant
everything turning to gold
in the vintage of the year
the mellow sun
falling on the harvest
and i think about you
& your blondness
like a dull sun
and how good it was
standing in your light

Before the Dawn
September 2, 1997

5:00 a.m.

unseen animals
slink by
in the darkness

tail end
of the summer . . .
air
warm
heavy
humid
but fresh
after yesterday's
many rains

no one else
abroad
only the crickets
sounding
the eternal background
of the universe

Baseball Field

July 13, 1997

summer sunlight
falls across
the empty
baseball field
waiting
for the potential game

falls on
the mathematical symmetry
of the loose-dirt
diamond inset
and on the white-powder
foul lines
radiating
into the clean distances
of outfield pastures

standing behind the backstop
in the shade
of a huge maple
looking down
the third-base line
i feel the alternating energies
of outward extension
and inward focus

New York City

you come in from somewhere
on a train
to the great mecca sanctuary
of the disaffiliated ...
of those who cannot conform
to the american shopping center
way of life

through hordes of people
moving in every possible direction
you make your way
to the token booth
through the turnstiles
downstairs
to the express train
(waiting for the local)

all seats taken
a few persons propped leisurely
against closed doors
the solitary maniac
blocking the doorway
looking up and down the platform

the local pulls in
an exchange of people
the doors close
and you're in it
the secret bowels of it

new york moves underground

June 21st

friday evening
first night of summer
graduation celebrations
cross our path . . .
the natural gaiety
of the teenyboppers
is slightly tinged
by the solemn realization
of transition

my friend & i
sit in the green environs
of the impeccable patio
in the wonderful balance
between stone & plant
art & nature
masculine & feminine

our toasts
are to the beginning
of summer
to the long days
stretching far ahead

ANGELINA'S RESTAURANT
6/5/02

the owner
a native of Naples
is under five feet tall
but as formidable
as a lion . . .
the kitchen help
waitresses
and delivery men
all have an Italian connection

trattorias & pizza parlors
are a dime a dozen nowadays
but nothing should be taken
for granted
it's not that long ago
Italians were not
a widely accepted part
of the population

all that has changed . . .
Italians have played
a prominent role
in every facet
of national life . . .
genetically they are
thoroughly integrated . . .
their philosophy of life
mannerisms
& rough good-natured humor

is so much a part
of the culture
they seem to have replaced
the Anglo-Saxon underlay ...
we are all part-Italian now

other nationalities
can claim as much ...
the melting pot
with its public school system
and democratic philosophy
has done its incredible work
and the world itself
in these advanced days
of technology
is far more cosmopolitan

at night
the red-glow interior
creates its own intimacy
the families
with their pizza-loving children
are gone
the remaining businessmen
relax in conversation
after their meal
the high-school senior
who is a competent night manager
discusses racing cars
with his crony
while the evening
draws toward its conclusion

like my friend says
it's not a high-class place
but it's all you need

SAUGATUCK RIVER
(Westport Library/July)

as in Vermeer's
"View of Delft"
one confronts
a structured row
of town edifices
a long stone's throw away
on the opposite bank

beside the library's
brick walkway
the slender trunks
of locust trees
lean over the river
their branches
wafting in the breeze
like northern palms

the gaunt look
of extreme low tide
reveals portions
of the river's muddy bottom . . .
the thinned surface
mirrors the half-tone brightness
of a hazy sky
and closer to shore
the empty sockets
of windowframes
in a much-diminished version
of the old city of Delft

Gringo

festive mexican bands
oom-pah
happy dance tunes
thru the piped-in
speaker system
at the fast-food
Sierra Grille

southwestern
tex-mex style
in Westport Connecticut
latino rhythms
on the edge
of the white man's world

at the borderline
i order
a black bean burrito
& a coke
then settle back
to the music
& a pastel-colored mural
of cactus country—
a pre-packaged import
for americanos

CHANCE ENCOUNTER

walking the main drag
40,000 cars
from the opposite direction
roaring by me . . .
4 girls
younger than teenager
in single file
coming toward me
all incredibly thin
led by the tallest
who greets me
as they pass

who are they?
where do they come from?
where are they going?
what does it mean?
can it be
despite the incredible odds
that in the end
the victory will be ours?

Organic Market

the languages
of the world
express themselves
in the international jargon
of cookery
"paella" is Spanish
"arame salad" and
"stir-fried vegetables"
Japanese
"humus" & "sesame tahini"
Middle Eastern
and "tofu stroganoff"
is a hybrid
of Russia & the Far East

all are subsumed
under the common idiom
of health-food recipes
all are participants
in a united nations
of worldwide palates

the women
in the kitchen
had former lives
in Armenia Lebanon France
& elsewhere
their skills are derived
from the international inheritance
of foreign cultures
their expertise

is a synthesis
from the continents & islands
of the globe

on the local radio station
classical music plays
throughout the day
the level is high-toned
friendly
but tense
because this is a commuter town
& on the go

meanwhile
the ladies of the kitchen
work hard
every day
determined looks
on their faces
turn to smiles . . .
gypsy witches
brewing the secrets
of the world's cookery
in magical cauldrons

AFTERNOON GAME

(Harbor Yard Ballpark)

one out of four thousand
rooting for the opposition
i cheer home
the Camden Riversharks
in a tight 2-1 win
over Bridgeport

one kid
gets on my case
imitating my rooting
for one of the Riversharks
otherwise
the Bridgeport crowd
takes me in stride . . .
i end the game
sharing observations
with another fan
watching the final two innings
of the tense cliffhanger

Harbor Yard Ballpark

in and out
smokestack pillars
the rising moon
plays hide-and-seek

like a giant baseball
symbolizing the game
it watches over the action
a cosmic spectator
absorbed in human affairs

the ghostly ferry
makes its departure . . .
scoreless innings
proceed apace
while the moon
heavy with destiny
mounts higher
in the tideless sky

"Purple Feet"

six of us
in the back room
of the wine & liquor store
eating spaghetti lunch
& drinking wine ...
the weekly saturday gathering

the ring of chairs
makes a loose
geometric shape
in the subdued light
of the stockroom
converted to dining room

actors
in the impersonation
of the moment
we perform
the ritual of the feast ...
to the flexible structure
of the tribal activity
the individual occasion
perfectly adapts itself

EVENING POEM

late-afternoon
and evening sunlight
after a day and a half
of rain and grey skies

outside the restaurant's
back door
the Japanese kitchen helper
smokes a cigarette

i pass by
on my travels
and the greeting we exchange
is across a cultural sea
acknowledging the same sun
shining on both of us

THE INJURED SWAN

lay crippled
on the beach
in the morning sun
at the edge of the tide

wouldn't eat
the bread
i threw it

gathered strength
to drag itself
a few inches
convulsive movement
of beating wings
& craning neck
that left it motionless

in all the world
around it
only the pitiless
sea & sky
and the body
now a shackle
the spirit
beating to be free

DAWN

i start out before dawn
the Big Dipper
a giant question mark
overhead
& the tidal creek
a meandering mirror
under lonesome starlight

the wide margins
of the receded sea
are like the dawning edge
of consciousness
before the vast dreamlands
of uninhabited space

the wandering starts
glitter in procession
moving towards the brink of time
the sky lightens
in the east
& the physical world
reveals itself again:

woods
and a narrow headland
along a curving coast
jutting out to sea

A LOCAL MURDER

Scorpio comes …
Halloween
All Souls
& All Saints Day
and big-city violence
spills over
onto the main drag edge
of the quiet village
1:30 a.m.
a side street
frost night grip
of the jackal moon

beyond the town's awareness
(dreaming through the local affairs
of its day)
the explosion occurs unheard
some trouble-full matter
brought to a dreadful conclusion
and now
the sun of a new day
streams through the consciousness
of those who alone know
what really happened

November

waning half moon
floats beyond clouds
in the violet dawn

cold nights & mornings
hoarfrost on the ground
the shortening days
make summer's freedom
a memory

i check the roads
leading out of town
the escape routes
north south & west

waiting for the sun
to rise
perhaps i'm holed up here
for another winter

FROST POINT

three black fishermen
like the remnant
of some native tribe
are to be found
on sunny afternoons
fishing in the offshore waters
near Frost Point

spaced apart
on the rocky shore
they huddle over their work
& the light absorbs them

we pass them on our walk
sometimes a greeting
sometimes a nod of recognition
they are not always the same men
but always the same fragment
of a lost fishing tribe
stranded on the mesolithic shore

CLOUDS

torn masses
of cotton candy
white explosions
from a shotgun
grotesque masks
rorschach formlessness

aftereffects
of last night's
thunderstorm
ragged sojourners
from a lightning-
riven sky
stray thoughts
of a celestial mind

the morning was foggy
sprinkled with rain
but by noon
the sun blazed forth
& an endless procession
of broken clouds
was making caravan crossings
over blue deserts of sky

ANTIQUES STORE

May 21, 1997
New York City

in
funeral
fluorescent
light
the chinese vases
ornate tables
candelabra
& giant
porcelain statues
rest
in their places
& the years
pass by

outside
9:30 a.m.
rush & tear
of the city
in breezy
arrowshafts
of sunlight

time
thick as dust
settles
on the objects
(silent as the gods)
while the frenzy

of the moment
beats vainly
at the glass window
of their imperturbable
placidity

THRIFT SHOP

in the thrift shop
where the old
board games
sit on shelves ...
the instructions
& some of the pieces
missing
but the dice
thick perfect cubes
in pairs
2 red
1 white
wait for some
imaginary player
to resurrect
the game

PARK STATUE

the body of the dead ram
(skin emaciated
gaunt at the throat
death-woe look of agony
in the sightless eyes)
lies prostrate
in the thick-taloned grip
of two demon vultures
(huge shadowy wings upspread
fierce eyes fixed on the sky)
perched in proud possession
on the decaying carcass

BEARINGS

6:30 a.m.
May 27, 1997
Greens Farms, CT
Burying Hill Beach

split-in-half
moon
angled
over the water
75 degrees high
in the southern
part of the sky

low coast
of Long Island
wavers
between mirage
& visibility

sun slanting
thru threes
is hauling up
the fish
of a brand new day

THE CONFEDERATE EXILES

11/18/98

political boundaries
really didn't
mean anything
anymore
even when you crossed
the Rio Grande
heading south

only a direction
remained ...
you had become
the cause
you fought for
and now the gods
of a mythical south
beckoned you
beyond the manmade
borders
of your world

no longer
the defense
of a homeland
only the wandering now
out of Egypt
through the mesquite
and the chaparral
like the athabaskan tribes
before you

moving south
through the corridors
of Mexico

ALICE-IN-WONDERLAND STATUE

the rabbit
has just consulted his timepiece
the mad hatter
looks stark-raving mad
the cheshire cat
and the march hare
look on
while Alice sits enthroned
in buddha-like tranquility
on a giant psychedelic mushroom

oh lotus land
where the riddles of the universe
run together and intercept
and time leads backward
through a door in a garden
let me smoke one bowl
to distorted reality
let me write one poem
to the imagination run wild

BALLPARK

i see the lights
and the star-spangled
spectacle of the nation
as the train
rolled out of Bridgeport
i beheld
as in a illuminated vision
nighttime baseball
and the stadium
all lit up
green grass of the outfield
red clay infield
the diamond shape
the white bases
and a game in progress
in the heart
of a minor league city

Dawn

November 7, 1995
Greens Farms, CT

the night is almost over
the full moon
shines thru the banded cloud
over the dark
still waters
of the tidal creek

along the horizon
the sky reddens
and the outlines
and solid bulk
of the world
return to sight

i wander along the seacoast
coincident with the dawn . . .
from spectral dreams
i'm returning
out of the death of night
i'm being born again

The Old Barn

in a field of sunlight
an old barn
rickety door wide open
yawning rectangle of darkness
unrevealed interior

suggestive sunlight
falls on sagging boards
i stare at the dark entrance
in the field of light
i stare into the absence
of action

CHRISTMAS DAY

black shapes
of wild turkeys
5 or 6 of them
on the lawn
at the entrance
to the deep woods

sun unrisen
pond frozen
the road iced over
and inch or two
of snow
covering the forest floor

in the intersecting zone
between curiosity and fear
i pass among the turkeys
they make a path for me
and i maneuver on past them
with a flag of truce
waving in my heart

NOCTURNE

thru the high
uncurtained windows
elongated moonlight
spills across the long wooden table
bathes the works of Paracelsus
in silver alchemical light

outside
in dark woods
katydids chant repetitively
their rhythmic chorus
attuned to invisible pulsations

night deepens
the sleepers sleep on ...
below the woods
the incoming tide
swells the creek ...
on the table
the words of occult philosophy
lie unread
like unspent treasure

The Dream of the Soul

i had the recurrent dream
in one of its many forms
dream of the midwest college

walking all night
over mountainous terrain
emerging at daybreak
in a totally strange city
wonderfully exhilarated
at being beyond the parameters
of my former world

new acquaintances
show me around
i join in activities
possibility of acceptance
into a new life
and escape from the previous
familiar existence

DAWN

gradually
the sky
distinguishes itself
from the water
then the land
along the horizon's edge

tilted half-moon
night's remnant wanderer
afloat in the sky's blue sea

before anything
can happen
the sun
must rise

The Tiger Bowl Restaurant

the strange fish
float
in their underworld tank

red lacquer light
spreads a warm glow
on tablecloths
and cushioned booths

shrill feminine voice
wails unintelligible chinese
in the background

separate tables
in the back
and the black
swinging doors
leading to the kitchen
leading to the chinese interior

SEA-LIFE

that we don't contemplate
their death
with the same shock
as we do
that of land animals

that i can handle
without repugnance
the body remnants
of a crab
but the soft
warm-blooded carcass
of a bird
makes all the difference

we breathe air
they die in it
they're as foreign
as creatures
from outer space
and though maybe
we came from them
it's much too far away
and long ago
to remember anything about it

Metropolitan Museum of Art

i love to pass the time
in the long galleries
of the art museum
not knowing what the weather's like
wandering down hallways
of the unconscious mind
in the rarefied atmosphere
of the art treasure
in an ultimate reverence
for the material object

October 1st

i saw hay bales
lying
in a golden field
wet with morning dew
rectangular bundles
of perishable straw
spaced like islands
in a horse pasture
in a world
made of earth and gold

TO LIPSO NAVA

when the season ended
probably
you went back home
to Venezuela
to Maracaibo
perhaps
to play in some
South American league
where the warm days
last longer

for you
the changes in geography
the different cities
the different continents even

day by day
while i sit
turning the pages
of the calendar
who in the world
knows where you are

THE ATLANTIC LEAGUE

now
far from consciousness
embedded
in the stratigraphy
of time
the league lies dormant
under a dream
of snow

somewhere in sleep
a game is being played
but a thousand complications
block the way ...
the ticket office
proves elusive
a labyrinth of stairway
endlessly multiplies ...
the immediate experience
of a greenfield
and a thronging crowd
turns, illusory
behind every opened door

The Great Horned Owl

at dawn
i hear him
in the distance
in the deep woods
5 or 7
short rhythmical hoots
repeated at intervals

the instincts
know what he means
but the mind
fails to express it . . .
something about
night and the cold
ghosts and the moon
something
that's been watching
all the while
you were asleep

RAILROAD

in the middle
of nowhere
a lot of empty
Coke machines
and old Pepsi trucks
penned in a yard
down by the tracks

shaded
edge-of-town
rises up
from the embankment

the train travels
thru the county
of disuse
thru the dark
neglected
unconscious mind

QUEENTH MARKET

old Queenth Market
sits deserted
on New Haven Avenue
the local cornerstone
that once
held the community together

that strange name
Queenth
like queen
taken to the nth power
or like some word
in a magical vocabulary
suggesting something sinister

i saw it
while it was still alive
once or twice
passing through . . .
you expect a place
like that
to go on forever
then you realize
you were seeing
an old man
on his last legs

THE BARON'S PROPERTY
(Westport)

we wander the grounds
up hill
and down dale
thru woods ...
would-be caretakers
on a ruined estate

the curtainless windows
we survey wooden floors
and staircase
untrodden for decades

the buildings say
KEEP OUT
but the land itself
(with its walkways)
has reverted to the public

centrally located
hidden behind the main drag
it remains
strangely isolated
vanished in broad daylight
from the general consciousness

Villa Rosa
and the Poli Mansion
(Milford, CT)

some one
or some group
saw the sunny Mediterranean
here
and the Italian Riviera
and not
the rugged coastline
of southern New England
and the boulder-strewn beaches
of glacial Connecticut

and built
genuine mansions
with iron grillwork gates
and circular driveways
terracotta villas
with open colonnades
through which
glimpses of the sea
like in a Greek myth

across the way
the sharp familiar angles
and plain stern countenance
of Puritan settlement
grim stockades
lonely attics
eschewing all ornament
and luxury

DARIEN

we sit at a booth
in Post Corner Pizza
as if
in an Edward Hopper painting
and the rock 'n' roll
radio station
plays
and the shadows
of afternoon
fall
like the passing of time

we sit
in the american world
of an Edward Hopper painting
in the isolation
of an individual booth
and the moments
slowly gather
and dissipate
and the conversations
go on
at the far table
as we sit
in the corner shadows
silently regarding
the imperceptible
passage of time

Ballpark Elegy

the ghosts
of former games
hover about
the abandoned
baseball field
where the weeds grow
and the grandstands
fall to ruin
and the light towers
on old wooden poles
hemisphering the outfield
look down blindly

local teams
played here
competed with teams
from other towns and cities
men and women
ate from the concessions
rooted for their heroes ...
only the structure remains
still looking out
across the daytime field
on into the american night

THE SKUNK

has his life
prowling among the leaves
crossing front lawns
after midnight
in the absolute radiance
of the moon

built low to the ground
he waddles on four feet
has silky-black hair
and a jagged-white
lightning stripe
down the middle of his back

no one knows better
the smells of the earth
the rain-damp ground ...
slowly, haltingly
he lumbers over the land
a north american mammal
been here a long time

Sleep

the body relaxes and the mind loses track
of consecutive reality

darkness and oblivion follow ...
the mind slumbering beside the body

and then the mind rises up
while the body's still asleep
(and dressing in the dark)
takes off on a journey
and this is the dream

Nightscape

3 a.m.
main drag deserted
no day in sight

gentle breeze
sets wet leaves fluttering
fresh odors
rise from rain-damp ground

sunk in darkness
the world reverts to inaction
everything ruled by dream

The Charwoman

relax about midday

they stand around
on the veranda
smoking and talking
while across the way
the electrical vacuum
is being repaired

in angles of reflected sunlight
they stand at their ease
the feminine working class
in its moment of enjoying the day

North Meadow

great
slow-moving
broken masses
of low-lying clouds
shagging the night sky

twinkling constellations
pinned like jewelry
on the broad black heavens

furlongs of enchanted ground
bathed in bright ghost light

NOTHING DOING

the wind blew at the thin
stiff grasses
in the snow

the sun illuminated the whole lake
beaming warmly on the arches
of the old wooden bridge

the moment came to pass
bearing no consequence
only an invisible wagon
rolled over the bridge
bearing the sun

once more
the moment quavered
on the verge of a kiss
or was it just the wind
blowing in the aftermath?

The Pequot Motor Inn

all of life
has flowed
thru these rooms
stopped
and gone on its way

rising sun
slants against low brick buildings
across parking lot openness

out in back
acres of great swamp
lay unseen
since the time of the Pequot

TO A LIBRARIAN WHO LEFT HER JOB

somewhere else
the bright giggle
of your talk
will be heard
your extreme competence
attractiveness
and winning manner
will be seen and felt
while we remain here
with the echo
of your memory
and a silent protest
against the transiency
that moved you on

PREMONITION

i went outside
to look at the sun
but the undertaker
cast his shadow
across my path

he stood tall and gaunt
a decrepit man
in a black top-hat
smoking a cigarette
looking like the chill of winter
before summer has left the land

New Year's Day

all the lakes were frozen
the rocks (as if in position)
did not move
nor did the snow melt one inch

it being a holiday
hopefully everyone says things
a little differently
the families drew their members closer
the cold seemed to demand it

the sun
for whomever saw it
setting in the interlacings
of the bare branches
was a crowning glory

in some dark room
of childhood experience
where everyone's old man is winter
a clock had toppled
kicking over the calendar
ringing in a new year

New Creek

a creek
is local
goes unnoticed
by the general populace
is crossed
without comment
by the speeding motorist

a creek
is a back alley
known only
to the local residents
is the key
to the landscape
opening the door
to midnight adventure
moves silently
like the indian
away from the settlements

The Pequot Library

in the crystal morning
a forgotten moon

down by the iodine sea
sun stirs unseen depths

waiting for direction
i perch on the stone steps
of the library
watching tree shadows
splotch the sun-drenched lawn

BRIDGEPORT
HARBOR YARD STADIUM

river
dark and gloomy
as the Styx
the ferry
waits
beneath
monolithic stanchions
of the superhighway

necromantic clouds
billow ominously
from satanic smokestacks
in the near distance

a ballfield
is a green
and day-colored
conjuring ground
perfectly flat
precisely lined
opening out
to the immensities

full moon
is last to view
behind cloud and mist . . .
day passes into night
and the field—
artificially lit—
concentrates attention upon itself

THE LIVING ROOM

above the
piano keys
the open
sheet music
reclines
on its
wooden rest

gray light
falls through
tall
curtain-drawn
windows

in the
attic-like
clutter
of old lamps
and piled chairs
faded memories lie
without sequence

THE RETURN OF ANDY DIORIO

in the alembic
of the game
after many distillations
and calcinations
the tug of war
of varying fortune
had prepared me
for sublimation

for three days
scrawling on a scorecard
in Arabic symbols
i recorded each step
of the work
positions of the planets
changes in the lineup
a fossilized representation
intelligible only
to the learned
while the sun set
and the interior lights
blocked out the night

by the third day
i had become the matter
taken on the properties
of the thing itself
become so absorbed
in the outcome
that in the moment
of transmutation

i was carried
beyond myself
out of the ballpark
of my expectations
truly sublimed
in the tie-breaking
three-run homer
that was everything
i could have wished for

To Andy Paul

the nights
grow cold
days blaze
with sunshine
October approaches
and the League
continues on
into the playoffs
before smaller
and smaller crowds

in the high north
the final game
to break the tie

the long season
stretches back
for you
to Lehigh Valley
to last place
and a losing record . . .
rebirth in Bridgeport
has taken you
to the high
Palace of Dreams

Baseball Season

it was february 22nd
and they were loosening up
their arms
a righty and a lefty
two teenagers
tossing a ball back and forth
with the easy motion
of the baseball player

the sun
shone down on the field
thru bulky white clouds
while i sat on a bench
off to one side
watching the old tradition
being carried on
and the slow return of the season

To Lipso Nava

to play baseball
one goes north
to Mexico
or Los Estados Unidos
where the big leagues
and the big money
and the origins
of the game
are to be found

traveling
between the small towns
and big cities
where baseball
is the common denominator
one gets to see the world

in the off-season
it's back home
to Venezuela
to the land
the northerners never see
land that Bolívar set free
to Lake Maracaibo
and Caracas
and the ancient kingdoms
of the Chibcha
to the Río Orinoco
and the Amazonian jungles
in the heart
of the Southern Hemisphere

HARBOR YARD BALLPARK

2/1/02

around the curve

the train slows
and the wide arc
of green outfield grass
opens to view

white foul lines
converge in perfect symmetry
the diamond-shaped in-field
and contoured strips
of expanding out-field
remain as relics
of an ancient agrarian system

in fallow-like repose
the field lies poised
between the buried moments
of a forgotten summer
and the long-awaited dream
of another season

EAST VILLAGE

i'm sitting
in Tompkins Sq. Park
in the warmth
of an early Spring sun
(declining in the west)
and a quarter-century has passed
since i lived on Tenth Street
with my girlfriend
between Avenues B & C
and anyway
i'm noticing everything
in a dreamy sort
of relaxation
come home to roost
for awhile
in the hippest place
the world will ever know

The Northern Artists

across the landscape of Holland
the seventeenth century moves
in the indubitable reality
of the peasant countryside
the traversable earth
has been set in motion
a distant church spire
beckons and guides ...
the solitary wayfarer
plods the open kilometers
between local villages
at the outskirts of which
chance encounters
tend to occur
at the intersection
of woodland paths

Nijmegen Castle

(after a painting by Jan van Goyen)

the patina of time
glints in sunlight
slanting on still waters
and weathered stone
trees sprouting from battlements
in shadowed recesses
under ivied walls
men with nets
and fishing boats
playing a desultory trade
on the river

Poem on Jan van Goyen's "River Scene"

sky equals
⅞ of the canvas
but you don't see it
at first
because the eye
is focused
at water level
and tilted upstream
where it meets
the full breadth
of the river
and the miniscule sails
afloat beneath
a cumulus-cloud sky

in the immediate foreground
men are breaching a rowboat
while in the near distance
atop the low incline
of the river bank
a horse-drawn cart pulls away
from a ramshackle tavern
another draws up to the entrance
and below
rowboats and sailboats
are docking or waiting
upon the long strip
of sandy shore
here is the eye
of the new science
more aware
of the curvature of space
here is the low-level view
of the Hollander
rescuing his stranded land
from water and sky

Southport
12/10/02

the trains
come & go
like acts of destiny

time converts
into distance

no particular place to go
i follow my usual way
under the RR tracks
into town

Harbor Yard Ballpark

12/12/02

rain puddles
and melting snow
leave the field
water logged

morning sun
streaks across
outfield grass

no game today
only an invisible ticket
or an indefinite future
to be purchased
by the passing spectator

MILFORD SHORELINE

12/12/02

wind rustles
thru dead vegetation ...
the vast theatre
of inactivity
surrounds me

only one pedestrian
in a five-mile zone
crossing the territory
ragged and low-lying

PALMIERI ROAD

i live
on a
one-street
dead end
going nowhere
along the creek
where it forms
a pond
back of the old mill

split-level homes
in monotonous ugliness
squared-out
of a former wilderness

a small refuge
circumferenced
by major roads . . .
the ecosystem
of the pond
operates unseen
even the waterfall
scarcely observed
by passing motorists

Fortune Cookie

we'd been passing
the chinese restaurant
for months
since the disastrous fire
wondering
if it would reopen
like the sign promised
when a car
pulling through the parking lot
of the shopping center
honked at us
once—then twice
before we realized
it was the owner
Mr. Li
and his compadre
in the front seat

NEW YORK
4/2/03

visited the big city
talk was all about the war
and terrorism—

in the park
clusters of daffodils
on reviving slopes
and trees starting to bloom—

by noon
inside the monumental hallways
of the art museum
wandering past the torsos
of ancient Greek statuary
i sat down to write
this paean
to my native town

To Lipso Nava

baseball
is a bridge
between continents
when i speak to you
before the game
and wish you good luck

each year
more than 7 months
go by
over 7 months
between Bridgeport
and Maracaibo
till i get
to see you again

this is the sixth year
of the League
as i stand
looking out
from the rightfield stands
into the westering sun—
old time traveler
bringing round
the slow cycle
of your return

WESTERN PAINTING

the viewer
squarely confronts
the back
of the last car
of a train
moving slowly
downgrade
away from him

in the near distance
(already dissolving)
a billow
of thick black smoke
rises skyward
from the locomotive

the yellow glare
of a hot
desert land
glints
from ridge rock
and broken
clay-colored
sandy
terrain

straddling the caboose
seven riders
unobserved
with Indian-black

pigtails
and high-domed
western hats
silently follow the train

one rider
leaning from his horse
grabs the railing
of the caboose
in the act
of boarding

in the reality
outside the picture
the viewer
(as unobserved
as the riders)
follows the action
of a holdup
forever about to occur

Harbor Yard Ballpark

and when they're away
playing in some other town
the home ballpark sleeps
in its own silence
mulling over
games soon forgotten
by an absent populace
returned to reality

the excitement
& the boredom
of the recent past
have balanced out
and the stadium
is returned
to its original stasis
to a mythical period
preceding creation

```
              C
              O
              N
              N
S  H  O  R  E  L  I  N  E
              C
              T
              I
              C
              U
              T
```

MILFORD POINT

through the centuries
down from Canada
pilgrimaging indians
to visit
the shrine of the ancestors
at Milford Point

forest-clad
mountains
become
lagoons
marsh grasses
gulf waters

stranded in this world
each one
on a Milford Point
the end drowned in the beginning

NATIONAL WILDLIFE REFUGE
MILFORD POINT

in the end
the wind
the earth
the sea
the sky

4 quarters
to the circle
that is
the world

quadrant in hand
man
overlooks the globe

FORT TRUMBULL BEACH
Milford

first memories
are
by the sea

things
lying
on a beach

clean slate
of wave
& water

horizon
empty
of all
earthly concerns

MYRTLE BEACH
Milford

so lonely by the sea
i gaze at the telephone pole mast

(lone totempoles of the coastline)
tilted against the western sky

WALNUT BEACH

Milford

gulls perch
on old remaining posts
crookedly set
in the low surf
like headstone markers
of the defunct Soundview Hotel

paint chipped & peeling
from white stucco walls
metal of beach chairs
rusting on the unused sundeck
no cars
in the wide driveway
of the once-gala Emerald Room

slowly crumbling
stone & concrete foundations
of the sea wall
exposed in the ebbing tide

COMPO BEACH

Westport

clouds bank
on the eastern horizon
under a hot morning sun

spit of wooded shoreline
like an island paradise
in the dreamy distance

circles & meridians
of sea-level geography
amid the vast calm of eternity

COMPO BEACH
Westport

potent dreams
from the timeless past
linger
in the cloud-blanketed morning

the exits
& entryways
between worlds
remain shrouded in mystery

down by the beach
the waters of a forgotten sea
lap upon the shore

COMPO BEACH
Westport

in the cold palace of dawn
the moon high in the west window
& the outlying territories
scattered beyond the sea
i stood on the veranda
of the beach
watching the shade-drawn sun
in the gathering east

FAIRFIELD

long warehouse sheds
just like isolated fingers
onto the edge of the marshes

the flattened landscape
becomes abstract distance

premonitions of the sea
draw the roving eye
shorewards
past solitary trees

PINE CREEK

Fairfield

in the warm
early october
sunlight
i sit watching
the zigzag meanders
of the creek
traverse the saltmarsh meadows
of the open floodplain
i gaze
at the bordering trees
on the opposite bank
wafting
in the gentle offshore breeze
and the world fades away
and from the half-remembered past
i look out
at woods
& a riverbank
& distance
i seem to have known
a long time ago

SOUTHPORT

10:00 p.m. churchbells
toll
in the humid night air

veiled half-moon
floats
in the southern sky

no wind
only the crickets stir

and down the track
the occasional hammering
of the railroad crew
working on into the night

MILFORD

the town sleeps
in mid-afternoon quiet

american flags
droop
from column & porch

out of sight
ten minutes walk
waters of the sea
the life of crabs
dreams below the conscious mind

GRAY'S CREEK
(Westport)

down by gray's creek
in the painted sunset
(the greater world
reflected in the lesser)
the peace of evening
descends
over the marshes
the silver wake
of the ducks
paddling homewards
dissolves
in the mirror of time
and ...

LOWER BURIAL GROUND

the lower burial ground remains
but not the church
which stood in the open field
across the road
burnt by the British
back in Hezekiah Ripley's time
he was minister then
church of christ congregationalists
old puritan stock

the sun wakens
on the headstones
of those who waken no more
slabs of stone
tilted and weathered
set in loose array
amid the straggling foliage
of a rambling country churchyard

one group
of particular notice
the Sherwood clan
gathered together
in the shade
of a holly tree
in loving union
unto eternity

Farms

Upper Burial Ground

country
morning
stillness

sun
falls
on headstones
standing
in dignified rows
outside
the minister's window
listening to the sermon
in eternity

on a shady knoll
gripless death
lies in solemn repose
resting from life's labors

mounting the hill
with human slowness
i follow
in the track
of the sun
light of my thought
casts its fleeting shadow
on the huddled graves
as I travel on
through the vale of tears

BRIDGEPORT

there's always something
land's-end eerie
about the marshes
level monotony
of broad distance
and measureless sky
lonely gull cry
and crow call
and back of bridgeport
for instance
the white cylindrical tanks
of the oil refinery
like some futuristic civilization
landed on an uninhabited world

Horse Tavern Creek

a thin runlet
it meanders
beneath a RR trestle
(abandoned and falling to pieces)

a ditch in the earth
it parallels
the back of a warehouse

a microenvironment
of creek life
with miniature banksides
it disappears
thru a pipe
underneath pequot avenue

to emerge
in fullblown marshland
wriggling free
towards mill river harbor
and long island sound

SOUTHPORT

nothing disturbs
the nighttime quiet
of village streets
under the spell
of a late-rising
three-quarters moon

down at the end of willow
the incoming tide
washes against the stony shore

over the landless darkness
the pale-bright moon
sheds its serene radiance

The Egret

stands in Sasco creek
looking like an egyptian ibis
sacred hieroglyph
from an original marshland alphabet

wet nile mud ooze
lies exposed
in low tide
ankle-deep waters

and the egret
slender and elongated
purely white
with black markings
picks his way among the shallows
probing the creekbed with pointed beak
wading in placid pooltides
out in the horizontal landscape

SOUTHPORT
(the freight station)

in a field of weeds
by the RR tracks
all the wildflowers
are blooming
in the afternoon sun
bees and butterflies
float undisturbed
sipping the nectar
and i wander undisturbed
in the botanical kingdom
of the wayside
amidst the multi-colored gaiety
of the plant world's vagabonds

SOUTHPORT

sits behind its sea-walls
and its breakwaters
atop the long low projection
of sasco hill
and along the harbor-running road
up rose hill
and up main and center street
down quaint willow
like a country lane
with picket fences and hedges
and low stone walls
dead ending in the saltsea tang
of the sound

a retired village
sequestered in shade
set in the angle
of the rivermouth
along an indentation
of the shoreline
proprieties of the gentry
and old memories
of the coastal commerce
of a small
well-to-do
19th-century seaport

BRIDGEPORT

after the game
a huge moon
hangs like fulfillment
over the city

after the madness
the low marsh
of the tides . . .
return to normalcy
stillness

above
in the vacant blackness
the moon
proposes the ancient riddle
as i stand
on the empty platform
waiting for the last train out

SASCO CREEK

runs high
in woodland shades and
speckled sunlight
thru tall reedgrass
meandering to the sea

mystery of water's movement
river deep as philosophy
moves in place
what is a river
what deep principle
do we recognize in it

in the presence
of its movement
standing on a bankside
looking out by day
across the land's low profile
or at night
moonrise over the river
the crab crawls forth
the journey is dark and unknown

The Carousel Thrift Shop

an afternoon
in time
the objects
sit on the shelves

miscellaneous
rarities
oddities
commonplaces

something to catch the eye
attract the heart
puzzle the brain

hangar racks of clothing
old post cards and records
debris from the world round

washed ashore
bits of culture
isolated artifacts

turning up from the grab-bag world

THE QUEEN OF SOUTHPORT

they give you a vacation
but you stay in town . . .
i pass you in the morning
coming out of the post office
i'm so madly in love
i can't help finding you out

queen of cups
blonde hair falls thick
and mane-like
abstractly you gaze
at the chalice of love
the world looks back . . .
you are sweet and sad
quiet and real
and you reign supreme
in the kingdom of the heart

Saugatuck River/Westport Library

the children
with their supervisors
abandon the picnic table
and trundle down
to the stone-walled
river embankment
encountering two swans
working their way upstream
against the outflowing tide

presently the humans leave
returning to the library
and now an old man
the poet
takes their place
sitting on a stone bench
gazing upon the river

puffy clouds
after the rain
float off
thru soft-blue
noon-day skies
the hum of commerce
diminishes
to its midday pace ...
leaning over the bankside
the locust trees
contemplate themselves
in the watery mirror

Southport Harbor

September 14, 2004
(Ye Yacht Yard)

i sit posted
on a public bench
under a hazy sun
facing the rivermouth
in a cooling breeze
one week left to summer

scattered boats
sit idle
anchored at their buoys
a lone inland crow
caws overhead
at the edge of the sea
the breeze whips the flags
on the crosspiece yardarm
the tide runs out to sea
speeded by the wind

framed by the jaws
of the rivermouth
the Sound extends
into the distance
bathed in hazy light
far as the low outline
of scarcely visible Long Island

a moment of undisturbed respite
in which to feel

the infinitesimal passage
of time
and behold the permanent rocks
the twisting shape
of the last prolongation
of land
and the final stages
of the river
running to the sea
like the exitway
to infinity

SOUTHPORT HARBOR

September 16, 2004

(Ye Olde Wharf)

blown inshore
the high-tide
mid-day waters
half-submerging
bright-green
spartina grass
while the paler foxtail
remains dry just above
nodding in the undulating currents
of the breeze

boats rock at their wharf landings
to the rhythm of the tide
a majestic late-season sun
rules gloriously overhead
frolicsome boys
cavort and shout
at the edge of the rivermouth
swimming in great splashes
across its narrow aperture
from shore to shore

i sit on a flat boulder
at the edge of the water
my feet bathed
in the cooling surges
and recessions
of the sea/river water
the air fresh

the sun bright
some cumulus clouds
after last night's
grudging rain

the kayak man
paddles off
embarking on his voyage
the lone fisherman
mounted on a spectator's wharf
casts for his luck
a few others
dot the immediate landscape
here is where the landlubber's
journey ends
and the vacant horizon
extends like the unwritten future

SOUTHPORT HARBOR

(Ye Yacht Yard)

i look out across
the land's end flatness
the last spit
of sandy beach
and the white gulls
and blue waters
of the Sound
on the last day
of summer ...

fading out
in glorious
peace and quiet
soft sounds
of talk
by the waterside
and the tide
filling in
the harbor's basin
with shadow
slow-motion
mirage-like movement

tremorous reflections
of anchored boats
and the blue sky
strafed with random
cirrus paint strokes
while i sit

on a stone wall
above the water
level with land and sea
holding the circular world
in the perimeter
of my vision

SOUTHPORT HARBOR
September 22, 2004

dead-level with the tide
seated on a half-submerged rock
i look straight out to sea
through the opening
of the rivermouth

all is calm . . .
stasis of the tide
between inflow and outflow
the gull afloat
the fisherman
casting from the wharf's edge
the soft breeze
stirring the spartina grass
and the thin group
of exposed trees
on the opposite shore
at land's end

here are the geographical
beginnings and endings
of the continuous world
here is the marriage
between continent and ocean
at the edge of each
under a radiant sun
in the turning of the seasons
from summer to fall

SOUTHPORT HARBOR
September 24, 2004

high-noon churchbells
sound in the background
the tide is low
the lone fisherman
has clambered down
to the edge of the rocks
to do his casting
a warm sun
is softened by remnant haziness

the hurried motions
of the world
have come to rest
"a nice place to sit and think"
observes the fisherman
in our brief exchange
he wishes me a good day
as he departs

only the back-and-forth
volley of a tennis ball
from the well-groomed
country club
on the opposite bank
punctuates the stillness
and the lap of the water
against a boat dock
the occasional cry
of a gull

and a soft knocking
from the crosspiece yardarm
like an irregular pendulum
sometimes marking
sometimes missing its beat
in the general surcease
of activity

SASCO CREEK MARSHES
(March 30)

all winter no one
to observe you

last year's tree nests
long since blown away

afternoon sun grown hazy
arcs through bare branches

dead leaves & dried stalks
strew untrodden tousled ground

at the edge of ravaged woods
birdsong trills
the early notes of Spring

SPRING POEM
(for Gail)

it's been years
as you said in your letter
but you had heard
i was not well of late
and that you'd be passing by
this way
on Saturday (the jewish sabbath)
and would like to visit me
and yes it's been
well over a decade
since i've seen
any of my father's family
and you especially perhaps
the one i most need to see

maybe you are the Star woman
(elder cousin of mine)
pouring water from two urns
one onto the land
one into the river pool
healing day bright consciousness
with family past unconsciousness
kneeling nakedly
under the eternal stars
knee planted on the ground
one foot in touch with the stream

April 9th the date
still two weeks to Passover
and the full moon ...

today a day
of brightest sunshine
cloudless april-blue sky
and clean-sweeping breeze

birdsong and buds
and the bright colors
of daffodils and pansies
crows and dandelion
and new bright-green
tufts of grass

i've come out
onto the windswept marshes
to stroll across
the winter-dead
short stemmed
cowlick spartina grass
and walk among the tall
dried plumed
phragmites reeds
in anticipation of your coming
to stand in prayer
beside the ancient tidal creek
flowing downstream to the Sound
no humans ever encountered here
sometimes a solitary kayak
or two in tandem
or other paddled vessel
once in a great while
following the contour meanders
of an old Sasqua Indian creek

spring now fully healing
the winter-frozen earth
and the thought of your coming
subtly healing my years-long
wounded psyche ...
maybe you are even now
on the road
shortening the distance
between us
this glorious Sabbath day
meant to heal
the week's hurried busyness
shabat shalom
i greet you
and you answer
shabat shalom to you

Sasco Creek Marshes

primitive
half-aquatic
no-man's land
naturally diked
subject to the tides
exposed to the winds
forlorn even in bright sunlight

reeds
over fifteen feet tall
sheathed and plumed
like slender arrowshafts
staked in thick array
remnants of a standing army
quivering in the april sun

spongy turf
matted with cowlick spartina grass
band of the meandering creek
sea-level flatness
gaunt dead-limbed
candelabra-branched tree
perch for birds of omen
bordering woods
and empty spaces
in a houseless landscape

SASCO CREEK

downstream
the water creeps
and the snake-white
phantom fog
drifts up
into the woods
and across the marshes
like the ghosts
of history
departing

zenith-high
crescent-thick
the translucent moon
floats in sky-blue vaults
while up from the horizon
rise rose-emerald-yellow
illuminations of dawn

everything
is absolutely still
as i look out
from the bridge
below the highway
like a taoist monk
in a chinese landscape
lost in the revelation
of the world

SASCO CREEK

the sun is sinking . . .
a golden sheen
slanting through the foliage
and the shallow waters
of the creek
drain towards the Sound

a solitary duck
appearing round a bend
proceeds upstream
exploring the slack water
along the bank

the sun is slowly sinking
to melt again
into all the other days
that have ever been
and we are here
watching these things
that once upon a time
happened forever

APPENDIX: BIBLIOGRAPHY OF UNPUBLISHED WORK AND PAPERS OF JONATHAN TOWERS

Original work by Jonathan Towers is <u>Underlined.</u> Titles of separate essays and major subsections of essays are so indicated, but not chapters within essays. All other titles are in *Italics*.

Notebook A: Literary

Part One: The 19th-Century Novel and Short Story

<u>Heroine on the Move: A Study of *Tess of the D'Ubervilles*</u> (13 pages)

    The Road in Hardy

    The Woman and the Earth

    The Sources of the Tragedy

<u>Atmosphere and Environment in *The Return of the Native*</u> (3 pages)

<u>The Idler in W.D. Howells' *Indian Summer*</u> (6 pages)

<u>Scenes From an Opium Den: Double Consciousness in *The Mystery of Edwin Drood*</u> (8 pages)

<u>The Novels of Jane Austen</u> (15 pages)

    General Characteristics

    The Crucial Journey

    Emma

    The Element of Surprise

    The Unhealthy Relationship

    Mr. Woodhouse and Mrs. Bates

<u>Thoughts on 19th-Century American and British Fiction</u> (14 pages)

    Coopers Comic Eccentricities: Archibald Sitgreaves

    The Landscape of War: Topographical Space in the Civil War Stories of Ambrose Bierce

    A Dichotomy in American Literature

    Twain's River Books

    David Balfour: The Progress of the Hero

    The American Somnambulist: A Study of Two Short Stories

    William Austin's *Peter Rugg, the Missing Man*

    The Wind in the Rosebush

    Literature in Politics: Chester A. Arthur and American Realism

copied by Jonathan Towers (18 pages)

The Town and the Outlaw: *Night on Don Jaime Street,* essay by Jonathan Towers (8 pages)

Lin McLean's Honey-Moon by Owen Winster, hand copied by Jonathan Towers (23 pages)

The Rainmaker and the Cowboy: Owen Winster's *Lin McLean's Honey-Moon,* essay by Jonathan Towers (5 pages)

Research Notes on *Zane Gray: A Biography* by Frank Gruber (8 pages)

Research Materials on Ernest Haycox (29 pages)

Notebook D: Research on Poe, Bierce, and Fredric

Research Materials on *The Fall of the House of Usher* by Edgar Allan Poe

"The Fall of the House of Usher" or the Art of Duplication by Claudine Hermann and Nicholas Kostis. Photocopy (14 pages)

Poe's Strategy in "The Fall of the House of Usher" by Bruce Olson. Photocopy (4 pages)

Research notes on Poe (56 pages)

Ambrose Bierce and Realism by Howard W. Bahr. Photocopy (20 pages)

The Damnation of Theron Ware by John Henry Raleigh. Photocopy (20 pages)

The Damnation of Theron Ware as a Criticsm of American Religious Thought by Elmer F. Suderman. Photocopy (12 pages)

Poe's Conception of Incident and Tone in the Tale by Walter Blair. Photocopy (14 pages)

Notebook E: Research and an Essay on Mary Wilkins Freeman and the American West

Research Materials on Mary Wilkins Freeman (20 pages)

Mary Wilkins Freeman, essay by Jonathan Towers (5 pages)

Research Materials on *The West: Its Commerce and Navigation* by James Hall (7 pages)

Notebook H: _Four Nineteenth-Century River Journeys_
Essay by Jonathan Towers (49 pages total)

Introduction
James Hall's _Letters from the West_
Preface and Letter I
Letters II and III
Letter IV
Letter V
Letter VI
Letters VIII and IX
Letters X-XII
Letters XV-XVII
Letters XVIII-XXI
Robert Louis Stevenson's _An Inland Voyage_
End of Essay

Notebook J: Research on Ancient Greece (15 pages)

Glossary of Ancient Greek names and places
Tracings from Ancient Greek mythology (mixed in with Glossary)

Notebook L: Scrapbook on Colonial Era European arts and culture. Various sources (54 pages)

Notebook M: Research Material on Sheridan Le Fanu and the Gothic Novel

Research Material on Sheridan Le Fanu and the Gothic Novel (intermixed) (43 pages)
Pages ripped out from _Thomas Vaughan at Oxford_ by Mary J. J. Skrine (13 pages)

Notebook T: Research material on the Gothic novel, Sheridan Le Fanu, Edgar Allan Poe and Ambrose Bierce

Research notes on the Gothic Novel (24 pages)
Order and Sentience in "The Fall of the House of Usher" by Arthur Robinson. Photocopy (15 pages)

The Bitterness of Battle: Ambrose Bierce's War Fiction by Eric
Solomon. Photocopy (21 pages)

Collection of Loose Typed Essays by Jonathan Towers

Action by Night: From the first chapter: *Mouth of the Canyon* by Ernest Haycox, hand copied by Jonathan Towers (11 pages)

Toll Bridge by Ernest Haycox, hand copied by Jonathan Towers (20 pages)

Lonesome Ride by Ernest Haycox, hand copied by Jonathan Towers (21 pages)

The Landscape of a Western Short Story: *Lonesome Ride,* essay by Jonathan Towers (3 pages)

Wine on the Desert by Fredrick Faust (Max Brand), hand copied by Jonathan Towers (10 pages)

Emerson Hough's *Heart's Desire:* Revisit to Eden, essay by D.E. Wylder, photocopy (11 pages)

Commerce at the Heart's Desire: Chapter XIX of "Romance at the Heart's Desire" by Emerson Hough, hand copied by Jonathan Towers (12 pages)

Notebook G: Essays by Jonathan Towers, Research Materials

Civil War in the Far West: Lewis B. Patten's *"Death Rides a Denver Stage,"* essay by Jonathan Towers

From: *Man Outgunned, Chapter 1* by Lewis B. Patten, hand copied by Jonathan Towers (2 pages)

The Popular Western as American Literature: Gordon D. Shirreff's *Last Train From Gun Hill,* essay by Jonathan Towers (15 pages, with interruption)

The Beginning of a Western: Lewis B. Patten's *Man Outgunned,* essay by Jonathan Towers (5 pages)

Narrative Strategy in Lewis B. Patten's *A Killing in Kiowa,* essay by Jonathan Towers (4 pages)

Research Materials on *Don Quickshot of the Rio Grande* (1 page)

Covers of Westerns and pictures from the American West (5 pages)

The Study of a Western: Ernest Haycox's *The Drifter,* essay by Jonathan Towers (15 pages)

Research materials on Ernest Haycox (10 pages)

Notebook B: Essays and Research Materials on Western Literature

Commerce at the Heart's Desire: Race and Tolerance in Emerson Hough's Frontier Society, essay by Jonathan Towers (5 pages)

Bibliography of Western novels in Bridgeport Public Library

Research notes on Western literature (10 pages)

The Cowboy in the Dime Novel by Warren French. Photocopy (14 pages)

The Author by Stanley R. Davidson. Photocopy from *Montana: the Magazine,* Volume 23 (Spring 1973) (6 pages)

Research notes (5 pages)

The Formula in Cowboy Fiction and Drama by Mody C. Boatright. Photocopy from *Western Folklore,* April 1969 (10 pages)

The Western Story. Photocopy from *A Literary History of the American West.* (6 pages)

Ernest Haycox: A Study in Style. by Brian Garfiled. Photocopy; source unknown. (3 pages)

In the Mode of the Genre: B.M. Bower's *Trouble Rides the Wind,* essay by Jonathan Towers (8 pages with Endnotes)

Sweet Grass: Chapter One by B.M. Bower, hand copied by Jonathan Towers (6 pages)

Glossary of Western Expressions compiled by Jonathan Towers (16 pages)

Pictures and Drawings of the American West, collected by Jonathan Towers (15 pages)

Notebook C: Research Materials, Stories, and Essays

Research materials from *Western Stories: A Chronological Anthology* (ed. Jon Tuska) (30 pages)

High Wind by Ernest Haycox, hand copied by Jonathan Towers (20 pages)

The Easterner in Abilene: *High Wind,* essay by Jonathan Towers (7 pages)

Science at Heart's Desire by Emerson Hough, hand copied by Jonathan Towers (14 pages)

Skirmish at Dry Fork by Ernest Haycox, hand copied by Jonathan Towers (17 pages)

The Frontier Army and the Western Towns: *Skirmish at Dry Fork,* essay by Jonathan Towers (5 pages)

The Tin Star by John Cunningham, hand copied by Jonathan Towers (19 pages)

Technique in *The Tin Star,* essay by Jonathan Towers (2 pages)

Three-Ten to Yuma by Elmore Leonard, hand copied by Jonathan Towers (18 pages)

The Deputy and his Prisoner: Elmore Leonard's *Three-Ten to Yuma,* essay by Jonathan Towers (4 pages)

The Westernization of *The Cask of the Amontillado:* Max Brand's *Wine on the Desert,* essay by Jonathan Towers (5 pages)

Notebook I: Essays and Research Materials on Western Fiction

Glossary of Western Expressions, compiled by Jonathan Towers (2 pages)

The Beginnings of Cowboy Fiction by Mody C. Boatright. Photocopy (18 pages)

Research Materials on *Points West (1928)* (15 pages)

B. M. Bower's Pictorial Art: A Look at *Points West,* essay by Jonathan Towers (10 pages)

Research Materials on *The Phantom Herd* (2 pages)

The Motion-Picture Western: B.M. Bower's *The Phantom Herd,* essay by Jonathan Towers (8 pages)

Research Materials on *A Rider of the High Mesa* (4 pages)

Covers and pictures of the American West (6 pages)

Mulford and Bower: Myth and History in the Early Western by William A. Bloodworth Jr. Photocopy from *Great Plains Quarterly,* Spring 1981 (11 pages)

Research Materials on various topics and from various sources (7 pages)

Research Materials on *Hopalong Cassidy Sees Red* by Clarence C. Mulford, hand copied by Jonathan Towers (42 pages)

Notebook S: Research Materials and Essays on Haycox, Mulford, and Patten

Research Materials on *The Wild Bunch* by Ernest Haycox (25 pages)
From Black Butts to Owlhorn Hills: Ernest Haycox's *The Wild Bunch,* essay by Jonathan Towers (7 pages)
Continuation of Research Materials on *Hopalong Cassidy Sees Red* (from Notebook I) (28 Pages)
The Gambling Ethos in Clarence Mulford's Westerns, essay by Jonathan Towers (12 pages)
Riding Point: The Western and its Interpreters by Richard W. Etulain. Photocopy (5 pages)
Bibliography: Westerns by Lewis B. Patten, Research Materials on Patten (15 Pages)
Unearthing a forgotten Wester: Lewis B. Patten's *Five Rode West,* essay by Jonathan Towers (6 pages)
Fact or Formula in "western" Fiction by Levette J. Davidson. Photocopy from *Colorado Quarterly,* Winter 1955 (9 pages)

Notebook K: Research Materials on Western Fiction and Edgar Allan Poe

Research Materials on Western Fiction (13 Pages)
What Happens in "The Fall of the House of Usher"? by J. O. Bailey. Photocopy (21 pages)

Notebook O: The Confrontation Between the Western Town and the Outlaw

Doolin' Dalton by the Eagles (2 pages)
Research Materials on Western Fiction and Doolin' Dalton (13 pages)
The Confrontation Between the Western Town and the Outlaw, essay by Jonathan Towers (56 pages)
  Introduction: The Historical and Legendary West
  Part One: The Dalton Gang
  Part Two: The Kansas Cattle Town
  Part Three: The James Gang

Part Four: Virginia City, Montana

Part Five: Tombstone, Arizona

The Town and the Outlaw: Ernest Haycox's *Night on Don Jaime Street*, essay by Jonathan Towers (8 pages)

History Versus Myth: *John Ringo: The Gunfighter who Never Was*, essay by Jonathan Towers (8 pages)

Epilogue in Two Parts, essay by Jonathan Towers (17 Pages)

Reconciliation: Ray Hogan's *The Law and Lynchburg*

Showdown: John Cunningham's *The Tin Star*

Notebook R

Research Materials on Zane Grey (5 pages)

Last Train from Gun Hill, Chapter 6, hand copied by Jonathan Towers (8 pages)

Pages Ripped out of *Ernest Haycox* by Richard W. Etulain (24 pages)

Notebook U: Scrapbook on Alchemy and the History of Alchemy (200 pages)

Photocopies of original essays may be purchased from North Atlantic Books, either for publication or personal use. Please contact customer service at www.northatlanticbooks.com or write to the address on this book for details.

Jonathan Towers

Senior year, when Jon and I were elected co-captains of the track team, I always thought of Jon as the *real captain* and myself as his co-captain.

In the spring, there were several of us who alternated between the half-mile and the 440. But there was only *one* miler: Jon. He had a heavenly stride—by which I mean he drifted above the cinders. His arms bent at an exact ninety degrees and his hands and wrists loose, like wings, Jon ran as quietly as he talked. That last lap, the last quarter-mile, he received a palpable surge of energy. His thin, pale body was transformed. Just as everyone else was fading, Jon became twice as strong. He won, breathing normally, then walked away from the group, and paced back and forth, hands on hips.

In the fall season, we ran cross-country. "At home" in Van Cortlandt Park, toward the end of the two and one-half mile course, just before we came down out of the hills, there was a precipitous stretch. The slanted terrain was rough and rocky, and the trees and prickly scrub bushes grew right up to the edge of the dusty trail.

It was the part of the race where I felt most desperate and alone, hearing my own labored breathing and the thudding of my own footsteps. Suddenly, out of nowhere, someone materialized at my left shoulder. I knew it was Jon, "making his move." As he passed me going down the hill, he patted me gently on the back.

We burst out of the woods and into the final, flat stretch across the grass, toward a small grove of trees in the distance that marked the finish line. As I watched Jon thread his way through a dozen or so of the first runners to emerge into that open space, I always smiled, because that gentle tap on my back had reminded me that I still had the momentum to keep going.

That is how I remember Jon Towers.

—Neil Baldwin

Jonathan Towers was born on April 19, 1948, in New York City. He grew up at 96th Street and Park Avenue, and Central Park West and 90th Street, the surrounding areas of Central Park his domain. He attended P.S. 6 and Horace Mann School where he was both a street fighter and an outstanding athlete—a baseball shortstop, a football quarterback, a first seed in tennis tournaments, and co-captain of his high-school track team for which he ran the mile.

He was a child of the sixties, most of which occurred in the decade of the seventies. An itinerant scholar without portfolio, a wanderer and adventurer, an aficionado of the vision quest, he attended the University of Wisconsin at Madison, Colorado College in Colorado Springs, the University of Colorado at Boulder, Towson State outside Baltimore, and Hunter College in New York City, studying literature and anthropology, excelling everywhere but never completing a degree.

A few of his jobs are worth mentioning: tutor of Chicano youth in Boulder during the early 1970s; counterman and juice-maker at Food Liberation on Lexington Avenue in New York City during the late 1980s; and night watchman at the Pequot Motor Inn in Southport, Connecticut, in the mid-1990s. (In this book readers will find his poems in the Provençal style to prostitutes whom he encountered at the latter establishment.)

He habituated Van Cortlandt Park (where he once ran competitive track), Central Park, the Colorado badlands, the fields of Baltimore, and the marshes and libraries of Southport and Westport, Connecticut. He observed nature, read omens, cleaned up litter, and wrote poems and essays. He moved from New York City to Southport and then Westport for the final decade of his life, as he chose to be close to the site of the last major Indian massacre in

New England, to attend to its ghosts. Westport was also where he spent his first two childhood summers, a time beyond memory.

For many years, known locally as The Walking Man, he traversed Westport, Southport, and Green Farms, some of his hiking with fellow outlaw Rosemary James whom he presented to folks as a descendant of Jesse and Frankie.

He also hung out at The Driftwood café in Southport Center with the town elders: Ted Brown, Ray Prescott, David Squires, Tom Hughes.

A fan of the independent Atlantic League Bridgeport Bluefish, he attended their games, keeping score and befriending players.

He read and re-read his own eclectic list of classics, preferring Westerns, American Indian ethnographies, and lesser-known British novelists and poets. A bibliography of his unpublished papers and notebooks appears herein as an appendix.

He always thought that Charles Dickens' *Great Expectations* encompassed his life. In truth, he began as Pip and ended as the convict. There was an Estella and a Jaggers.

His father's surname was Turetsky, but he changed it in order to do business in Manhattan: impresario and adman.

Jonathan David Towers ended his own life on May 4th, 2005, by a knife.

Those interested in further details of Jonathan Towers' life and death and more of his words can investigate two books by his brother Richard Grossinger, *Out of Babylon: Ghosts of Grossinger's* (Berkeley, California: Frog, Ltd., 1997) and *On the Integration of Nature: Post-9/11 Biopolitical Notes* (Berkeley, California: North Atlantic Books, 2005).